Self-Assessment Library 3.4
Insights into Your Skills, Interests and Abilities

Stephen P. Robbins

San Diego State University

PEARSON

Prentice Hall

Upper Saddle River, New Jersey 07458

Editorial Director: Sally Yagan
Acquisitions Editor: Jennifer Collins
Editorial Project Manager: Claudia Fernandes
Senior Managing Editor: Judy Leale
Associate Managing Editor: Suzanne DeWorken
Operations Specialist: Carol O'Rourke

Pearson Prentice Hall™ is a trademark of Pearson Education, Inc.

10   9   8   7   6   5   4   3   2   1

ISBN-13: 978-0-13-608376-4
ISBN-10: 0-13-608376-5

Table of Contents

G. Other

*Instruments identified with this asterisk presume that the student completing the test is currently working. These can be omitted for students who are not presently employed.

Preface

Some truths stand the test of time. This applies to the statement made more than 2500 years ago by the Chinese philosopher, Lao-tzu: "He who knows others is clever; he who knows himself is enlightened."

The Self-Assessment Library has been created to help you to learn more about yourself so that you might become "enlightened." It draws on numerous instruments that have been developed by behavioral researchers that tap into your skills, abilities, and interests. This new edition has eighteen instruments that were not included in the previous version. This Library of behavioral questionnaires has been designed to supplement a wide range of college courses. These include: Introduction to Management, Organizational Behavior, Supervision, Human Relations, Interpersonal Skills, Introduction to Business, Careers in Business, Industrial and Organizational Psychology, and Social Psychology. It works best when questionnaires are completed separately (rather than doing the whole set at one time) and when they're completed in sync with text readings on complementary topics. For instance, the two instruments on communication skills are best completed when you're reading and learning about the topic of interpersonal communication. Please keep in mind that these instruments were designed to be used in conjunction with a textbook and are *not* meant to be stand-alone learning tools. Exhibit 1 provides a general guide to help you match up the instruments with relevant organizational behavior and management topics.

Exhibit 1- List of Self-Assessment Instruments by Topic

Topic	Requires Work Experience	CD Listing																	
		I.					II.			III.			IV.						
		A	B	C	D	E	A	B	C	A	B	C	A	B	C	D	E	F	G
Attitudes and job satisfaction	*		3	7															
Communication							1 2										3		
Conflict									5										
Creativity		5																	
Decision making					1								2						
Diversity			4												2				
Emotions						1										1 2			
Entrepreneurship						4													
Ethics					2												4		
General Knowledge																			1 2
Globalization											5								
Job design	*			8 9															
Job involvement	*		2												1				
Job satisfaction	*		3																
Leadership								1 2 5									4		
Managing change												1							
Managing conflict								5 6											
Motivation				1- 5							4								
Negotiation									6										

(Continues on next page)

Topic	Requires Work Experience	I. A	I. B	I. C	I. D	I. E	II. A	II. B	II. C	III. A	III. B	III. C	IV. A	IV. B	IV. C	IV. D	IV. E	IV. F	IV. G
Organization design										1									
Organizational change												1							
Organizational commitment	*										2								
Organizational culture											1								
Organizational design											1 2							2	
Performance feedback	*							3											
Performance reviews	*										3								
Personality		1 2 4		6											1 3 4				
Planning				5		2 3													
Politics	*							3 4										1	
Power								1 2											
Power and politics	*							1-4											
Productivity						2													
Teams								6									1 2		
The manager's job	*		2			1				2	4								
Trust								3 4											
Values			1												1			2	
Work stress	*	3									3	2 3							
Workplace diversity	*		4												2				

CD Listing

viii

I.A.1: What's My Basic Personality?

Instrument
Listed below is a set of 15 adjective pairs. For each, select the number along the scale (you must choose a whole number) that most closely describes you or your preferences.

1.	Quiet	1	2	3	4	5	Talkative
2.	Tolerant	1	2	3	4	5	Critical
3.	Disorganized	1	2	3	4	5	Organized
4.	Tense	1	2	3	4	5	Calm
5.	Imaginative	1	2	3	4	5	Conventional
6.	Reserved	1	2	3	4	5	Outgoing
7.	Uncooperative	1	2	3	4	5	Cooperative
8.	Unreliable	1	2	3	4	5	Dependable
9.	Insecure	1	2	3	4	5	Secure
10.	New	1	2	3	4	5	Familiar
11.	Sociable	1	2	3	4	5	Loner
12.	Suspicious	1	2	3	4	5	Trusting
13.	Undirected	1	2	3	4	5	Goal-oriented
14.	Enthusiastic	1	2	3	4	5	Depressed
15.	Change	1	2	3	4	5	Status-quo

_____

Source: Based on O.P. John, "The 'Big Five' Factor Taxonomy: Dimensions of Personality in the Natural Language and in Questionnaires," in L.A. Pervin (ed.), *Handbook of Personality Theory and Research* (New York: Guilford Press, 1990), pp. 66-100; and D.L. Formy-Duval, J.E. Williams, D.J. Patterson, and E.E. Fogle, "A 'Big Five' Scoring System for the Item Pool of the Adjective Check List," *Journal of Personality Assessment*, Vol 65, 1995, pp. 59-76.

Scoring Key
To calculate your personality score, add up your points as follows (reverse scoring those items marked with an asterisk):

> Items 1, 6, and 11*. This is your extraversion score.
> Items 2*, 7, and 12. This is your agreeableness score.
> Items 3, 8, and 13. This is your conscientiousness score.
> Items 4, 9, and 14*. This is your emotional stability score.
> Items 5*, 10*, and 15*. This is your openness-to-experience score.

Analysis and Interpretation
The five-factor model of personality—often referred to as the Big Five—has an impressive body of research supporting that five basic personality dimensions underlie human behavior. These five dimensions are defined as follows:

> **Extraversion** – Someone who is sociable, talkative, and assertive. High scores indicate you're an extravert; low scores indicate you're an introvert.

Agreeableness – Someone who is good-natured, cooperative, and trusting. This is a measure of your propensity to defer to others. High scores indicate you value harmony; low scores indicate you prefer having your say or way on issues.

Conscientiousness – Someone who is responsible, dependable, persistent, and achievement oriented. High scores indicate that you pursue fewer goals in a purposeful way; while low scores indicate that you're more easily distracted, pursue many goals, and are more hedonistic.

Emotional stability – Someone who is calm, enthusiastic, and secure. High scores indicate positive emotional stability, with low scores indicating negative emotional stability.

Openness to experience – Someone who is imaginative, artistically sensitive, and intellectual. High scores indicate you have a wide range of interests and a fascination with novelty and innovation; low scores indicate you're more conventional and find comfort in the familiar.

What defines a high or low score? No definite cutoffs are available. However, reasonable cutoffs for each dimension would be 12-15 points = high; 7-11 = moderate; and 3-6 = low.

The most impressive evidence relates to the conscientiousness dimension. Studies show that conscientiousness predicts job performance for all occupational groups. The preponderance of evidence indicates that individuals who are dependable, reliable, thorough, organized, able to plan, and persistent (that is, high on conscientiousness) tend to have higher job performance in most if not all occupations. In addition, individuals who score high in conscientiousness develop higher levels of job knowledge, probably because highly conscientious people exert greater levels of effort on their job. The higher levels of job knowledge then contribute to higher levels of job performance.

Other insights from your scores: High scores on extraversion indicate you may be suited to a managerial or sales position. These occupations require high social interaction. And high scores on openness-to-experience is a good predictor of your ability to achieve significant benefits from training efforts.

I.A.2: What's My Jungian 16-Type Personality?

Instrument

For each item, select either a or b. If you feel both a and b are true, decide which one is more like you, even if it is only slightly more true.

1. I would rather
    a. Solve a new and complicated problem.
    b. Work on something I have done before.

2. I like to
    a. Work alone in a quiet place.
    b. Be where the action is.

3. I want a boss who
    a. Establishes and applies criteria in decisions.
    b. Considers individual needs and makes exceptions.

4. When I work on a project, I
    a. Like to finish it and get some closure.
    b. Often leave it open for possible changes.

5. When making a decision, the most important considerations are
    a. Rational thoughts, ideas, and data.
    b. People's feelings and values.

6. On a project, I tend to
    a. Think it over and over before deciding how to proceed.
    b. Start working on it right away, thinking about it as I go along.

7. When working on a project, I
    a. Maintain as much control as possible.
    b. Explore various options.

8. In my work, I prefer to
    a. Work on several projects at a time, and learn as much as possible about each one.
    b. Have one project that is challenging and keeps me busy.

9. I often
    a. Make lists and plans whenever I start something and may hate to seriously alter my plans.
    b. Avoid plans and just let things progress as I work on them.

10. When discussing a problem with colleagues, it is easy for me to
    a. See "the big picture."
    b. Grasp the specifics of the situation.

11. When the phone rings in my office or at home, I usually
    a. Consider it an interruption.
    b. Do not mind answering it.

12. Which word describes you better?
    a. Analytical.
    b. Empathetic.

13. When I am working on an assignment, I tend to
    a. Work steadily and consistently.
    b. Work in bursts of energy with "down time" in between.

3

14. When I listen to someone talk on a subject, I usually try to
    a. Relate it to my own experience and see if it fits.
    b. Assess and analyze the message.
15. When I come up with new ideas, I generally
    a. "Go for it."
    b. Like to contemplate the ideas some more
16. When working on a project, I prefer to
    a. Narrow the scope so it is clearly defined.
    b. Broaden the scope to include related aspects.
17. When I read something, I usually
    a. Confine my thoughts to what is written there.
    b. Read between the lines and relate the words to other ideas.
18. When I have to make a decision in a hurry, I often
    a. Feel uncomfortable and wish I had more information.
    b. Am able to do so with available data.
19. In a meeting, I tend to
    a. Continue formulating my ideas as I talk about them.
    b. Only speak out after I have carefully thought the issue through.
20. In work, I prefer spending a great deal of time on issues of
    a. Ideas.
    b. People.
21. In meetings, I am most often annoyed with people who
    a. Come up with many sketchy ideas.
    b. Lengthen meetings with many practical details.
22. I am a
    a. Morning person.
    b. Night owl.
23. What is your style in preparing for a meeting?
    a. I am willing to go in and be responsive.
    b. I like to be fully prepared and usually sketch an outline of the meeting.
24. In a meeting, I would prefer for people to
    a. Display a fuller range of emotions.
    b. Be more task oriented.
25. I would rather work for an organization where
    a. My job was intellectually stimulating.
    b. I was committed to its goals and mission.
26. On weekends, I tend to
    a. Plan what I will do.
    b. Just see what happens and decide as I go along.
27. I am more
    a. Outgoing.
    b. Contemplative.
28. I would rather work for a boss who is
    a. Full of new ideas.
    b. Practical

In the following, choose the word in each pair that appeals to you more:
  29.   a. Social.
         b. Theoretical.
  30.   a. Ingenuity.
         b. Practicality.
  31.   a. Organized.
         b. Adaptable.
  32.   a. Active.
         b. Concentration.

_____

Source: D. Marcic and P. Nutt, "Personality Inventory," in D. Marcic, ed., *Organizational Behavior: Experiences and Cases* (St. Paul, MN: West, 1989).

Scoring Key

Score this test as follows: Count one point for each item listed below that you have marked in the inventory.

	Score for I	Score for E	Score for S	Score for N
	2a	2b	1b	1a
	6a	6b	10b	10a
	11a	11b	13a	13b
	15b	15a	16a	16b
	19b	19a	17a	17b
	22a	22b	21a	21b
	27b	27a	28b	28a
	32b	32a	30b	30a
Total	___	___	___	___

Identify the one with the more points--I or E.

Identify the one with the more points--S or N.

	Score for T	Score for F	Score for J	Score for P
	3a	3b	4a	4b
	5a	5b	7a	7b
	12a	12b	8b	8a
	14b	14a	9a	9b
	20a	20b	18b	18a
	24b	24a	23b	23a
	25a	25b	26a	26b
	29b	29a	31a	31b
Total	___	___	___	___

Identify the one with the more points--T or F.

Identify the one with the more points--J or P.

Now combine your score into a four-letter personality classification.

Analysis and Interpretation

This questionnaire classifies people as extroverted or introverted (E or I), sensing or intuitive (S or N), thinking or feeling (T or F), and perceiving or judging (P or J). These classifications can then be combined into 16 personality types (for example, INTJ, ENTP).

Find your personality, interpretation, and possible career choices* from the following:

ISTJ. You're organized, compulsive, private, trustworthy, and practical. Possible career as office manager, accountant, business manager, tax agent, public servant.

ISFJ. You're loyal, amiable, and willing to make sacrifices for the greater good. Possible career as masseur, vet, painter, mechanic, clerical supervisor.

INFJ. You're reflective, introspective, creative, and contemplative. Possible career as psychologist, librarian, drama teacher, novelist, human resources manager.

INTJ. You're skeptical, critical, independent, determined, and often stubborn. Possible career as a business analyst, environmental planner, lawyer, reporter, engineer, scientist.

ISTP. You're observant, cool, unpretentious, and highly pragmatic. Possible career as a commercial artist, racing-car driver, chiropractor, firefighter, pilot.

ISFP. You're warm, sensitive, unassuming, and artistic. Possible career as landscape architect, botanist, science teacher, fashion designer, interior designer.

INFP. You're reserved, creative, and highly idealistic. Possible career as architect, journalist, educational consultant, missionary, actor, artist, poet.

INTP. You're socially cautious, enjoy problem solving, and highly conceptual. Possible career as plastic surgeon, software designer, psychoanalyst, private investigator, financial analyst, mathematician, photographer.

ESTP. You're outgoing, live for the moment, unconventional, and spontaneous. Possible career as stockbroker, insurance or car salesperson, bartender, sports coach, entertainment promoter.

ESFP. You're sociable, fun-loving, spontaneous, and very generous. Possible career as a events coordinator, musician, ER nurse, fund-raiser, comedian.

ENFP. You're people-oriented, creative, and highly optimistic. Possible career as publicist, research assistant, playwright, restaurateur, columnist, conflict mediator.

ENTP. You're innovative, individualistic, versatile, and entrepreneurial. Possible career as politician, strategic planner, literary agent, publicist, entrepreneur, investment broker, computer analyst, ad executive.

ESTJ. You're realistic, logical, analytical, decisive, and have a natural head for business or mechanics. You like to organize and run things. Possible career as corporate executive, medical technologist, curator, health-care administrator, teacher, dentist.

ESFJ. You're gracious, have good interpersonal skills, and are eager to please. Possible career as social worker, optometrist, childcare worker, nun.

ENFJ. You're charismatic, compassionate, and highly persuasive. Possible career as a TV producer, fundraiser, drama teacher, health adviser.

ENTJ. You're outgoing, visionary, argumentative, have a low tolerance for incompetence, and often seen as a natural leader. Possible career as a manager, management trainer, stockbroker, lawyer, chemical engineer, police officer.

*Career suggestions offered by M. Eggert, *The Best Job-Hunt Book in the World* (New York: Random House, 2000).

What value can this personality classification provide you? It can help you understand your personality--your strengths and your weaknesses. It can help you in making successful career decisions when you try to find jobs that align well with your strengths and avoid those jobs that are a poor fit.

I.A.3: Am I a Type-A?

Instrument

Identify the number on the scale that best characterizes your behavior for each trait. You must choose a whole number. Be sure to move each slider before you calculate.

1. Casual about appointments	1 2 3 4 5 6 7 8	Never late
2. Not competitive	1 2 3 4 5 6 7 8	Very competitive
3. Never feel rushed	1 2 3 4 5 6 7 8	Always feel rushed
4. Take things one at a time	1 2 3 4 5 6 7 8	Try to do many things at once
5. Slow doing things	1 2 3 4 5 6 7 8	Fast (eating, walking, etc.)
6. Express feelings	1 2 3 4 5 6 7 8	"Sit on" feelings
7. Many interests	1 2 3 4 5 6 7 8	Few interests outside work

Source: Adapted from R.W. Bortner, "Short Rating Scale as a Potential Measure of Pattern A Behavior," *Journal of Chronic Diseases*, June 1969, pp. 87-91. With permission.

Scoring Key

To calculate your score, total up your numbers on the seven questions. Now multiply by 3.

Analysis and Interpretation

This instrument measures the degree to which you're competitive and rushed for time. The Type A personality describes someone who is aggressively involved in a chronic, incessant struggle to achieve more and more in less and less time. More specifically, Type As are always moving, walking, and eating rapidly; feel impatient with the pace of most events; strive to do two or more things at once; do not cope well with leisure time; and are obsessed with numbers, measuring their success in terms of how many or how much of everything they acquire. Type As have a strong need to get a lot done in a short time period and can be difficult to get along with because they are so driven. They're not particularly good team players. They also often interrupt other people and even finish others' sentences because of their impatience. In contrast, Type Bs are the exact opposites.

A total of 120 or more indicates that you are a hard-core Type A. Scores below 90 indicate that you are a hard-core Type B. The following gives you more specifics:

120 or more points	=	A+ personality type
106-119	=	A
100-105	=	A-
90-99	=	B+
Less than 90	=	B

If you score in the "A" categories, you need to be aware of your tendency to focus on quantity over quality. You may do better in jobs that are routine and rely on speed rather than creativity for success. You are also probably better matched to jobs where you can work alone rather than on teams. And recognize that you may become frustrated working on long-term projects because of your need to see results. Finally, Type As often experience moderate to high levels of stress. So if you're a hard-core Type A, identify stress-management techniques that work for you and use them. It might just save you from a heart attack.

I.A.4: How Well Do I Handle Ambiguity?

Instrument

Respond to each of the statements by indicating the extent to which you agree or disagree with them. Use the following rating scale for your responses:

    1 = Strongly agree
    2 = Moderately agree
    3 = Slightly agree
    4 = Neither agree or disagree
    5 = Slightly disagree
    6 = Moderately disagree
    7 = Strongly disagree

1. An expert who doesn't come up with a definite answer
   probably doesn't know too much.   1 2 3 4 5 6 7
2. There is really no such thing as a problem that can't
   be solved.   1 2 3 4 5 6 7
3. A good job is one in which what is to be done and
   how it is to be done are always clear.   1 2 3 4 5 6 7
4. In the long run, it is possible to get more done by
   tackling small, simple problems than large and
   complicated ones.   1 2 3 4 5 6 7
5. What we are used to is always preferable to what
   is unfamiliar.   1 2 3 4 5 6 7
6. A person who leads an even, regular life in which
   few surprises or unexpected happenings arise
   really has a lot to be grateful for.   1 2 3 4 5 6 7
7. I like parties where I know most of the people more
   than ones where all or most of the people are
   complete strangers.   1 2 3 4 5 6 7

Source: M. J. Kirion, "A Reanalysis of Two Scales of Tolerance of Ambiguity," *Journal of Personality Assessment*, August 1981, pp. 407-14. Adapted from S. Budner, "Intolerance of Ambiguity as a Personality Variable," *Journal of Personality*, March 1962, pp. 29-50.

Scoring Key

To score your answers, merely sum up the total on the seven items.

Analysis and Interpretation

Having intolerance of ambiguity means that you tend to perceive situations as threatening rather than promising. You prefer more structured situations. In contrast, people who score high on tolerance respond better to change and new situations.

Your score will fall between 7 and 49. People with higher scores are tolerant of and even enjoy ambiguous situations. People with low scores are intolerant of ambiguity. Extrapolating from research findings suggest that people will typically score between 10 and 35, with a mean around 20.

In today's dynamic work environment, where changes occur at an ever faster pace, the ability to tolerate ambiguity becomes a valuable asset. A high tolerance for ambiguity makes you more likely to be able to function in a work world where there is less certainty about expectations, performance standards, and career progress. If you're intolerant of ambiguity, it's OK. But you should organize your life and seek career options that fit with your need for clarity and structure.

I.A.5: How Creative Am I?

Instrument
Review the 30 adjectives on your right. Being honest and forthright with your answers, identify only those items that accurately describe you.

1. affected	11. honest	21. reflective
2. capable	12. humorous	22. resourceful
3. cautious	13. individualistic	23. self-confident
4. clever	14. informal	24. sexy
5. commonplace	15. insightful	25. sincere
6. confident	16. intelligent	26. snobbish
7. conservative	17. inventive	27. submissive
8. conventional	18. mannerly	28. suspicious
9. dissatisfied	19. narrow interests	29. unconventional
10. egotistical	20. original	30. wide interests

_____

Source: H.G. Gough, "A Creative Personality Scale for the Adjective Check List," *Journal of Personality and Social Psychology*, August 1979, pp. 1398-1405.

Scoring Key
To calculate your score, give yourself +1 if you described yourself using items 2, 4, 6, 10, 12, 13, 14, 15, 16, 17, 20, 21, 22, 23, 24, 26, 29, and 30. Give yourself a -1 for any of the remaining items which you said accurately described you.

Analysis and Interpretation
Creativity is the ability to combine ideas in a unique way or to make unusual associations between ideas. A creative person develops novel approaches to doing their work or unique solutions to problems.

This questionnaire was developed to identify creative talent and potential. It has been widely used and replicated. It is composed of 30 items--18 of which have been found to be positively associated with creativity, and 12 that are negatively correlated. Your score will range between -12 and +18. The higher your positive score, the more you display characteristics associated with a creative personality.

For managers, creativity is useful in decision making. It helps them to see problems and alternatives that others might not. All jobs, of course, don't require high creativity. And highly creative individuals, when faced with routine and structured jobs, often become frustrated and dissatisfied. If you score high on creativity, you should ideally seek a job that will provide you with a creative outlet. If that's not possible, utilize your free time to develop hobbies and interests that can satisfy your need for creative expression. If you're interested in trying to improve your creativity, you might find the following books helpful: W.J.J. Gordon, *Synectics: The Development of Creative Capacity* (Harper & Row, 1961; R. Von Oech, *A Whack on the Side of the Head* (Warner, 1983); T. Wujec, *Five Star Mind: Games & Exercises to Stimulate Your Creativity and Imagination* (Main Street Press, 1995); and J.E. Ayan, *Aha! Ten Ways to Free Your Creative Spirit & Find Your Great Ideas* (Crown Books, 1997).

I.B.1: What Do I Value?

Instrument

Listed are two sets of statements. The first list presents 10 terminal values. These are desirable end-states of existence. Think of them as goals that you might like to achieve during your lifetime. The second list presents 10 instrumental values. These are preferable modes of behavior, or means of achieving the terminal values.

For each list, rank the statements according to how important each is to you personally. Score a "1" next to the value that is most important, a "2" next to the second most important, and so forth. Treat each list separately.

Terminal Values

____ Happiness; satisfaction in life
____ Knowledge and wisdom
____ Peace and harmony in the world
____ Pride in accomplishment
____ Prosperity; wealth
____ Lasting friendships
____ Recognition from peers
____ Salvation; finding eternal life
____ Security; freedom from threat
____ Self-respect

Instrumental Values

____ Assertiveness; standing up for yourself
____ Being helpful or caring toward others
____ Dependability; being counted upon by others
____ Education and intellectual pursuits
____ Hard work and achievement
____ Obedience; following the wishes of others
____ Open-mindedness; receptivity to new ideas
____ Self-sufficiency; independence
____ Truthfulness; honesty
____ Being well-mannered and courteous toward others

_____
Source: Based on M. Rokeach, *The Nature of Human Values* (New York: Free Press, 1973).

Analysis and Interpretation

Values are basic convictions of what is right, good, or desirable. Your values reflect what you think is important. There are, of course, no right or wrong values. This self-assessment merely gives you some directive insights into your value structure.

Research demonstrates that people in the same occupation tend to hold similar values. For instance, a study of corporate managers found that they ranked self-respect and security as their top rated terminal values. For instrumental values, these same corporate managers rated truthfulness first, followed by dependability.

It may be helpful to assess your value structure in terms of your career aspirations. Specifically, to what degree do you think your values align with those of successful people in the field to which you aspire? And what conflicts, if any, do you see between your values and the values espoused by people in the field in which you aspire to work? Do you think you are able to reconcile those conflicts?

I.B.2: How Involved Am I in My Job?

Instrument

This test contains ten statements each of which you may agree or disagree with depending on your personal evaluation of your present job. Please indicate the degree of your agreement or disagreement with each statement using the following scale:

        1 = Strongly disagree
        2 = Disagree
        3 = Mildly disagree
        4 = Mildly agree
        5 = Agree
        6 = Strongly agree

1. The most important things that happen to me involve my present job.	1	2	3	4	5	6
2. To me, my job is only a small part of who I am.	1	2	3	4	5	6
3. I am very much involved personally in my job.	1	2	3	4	5	6
4. I live, eat, and breathe my job.	1	2	3	4	5	6
5. Most of my interests are centered around my job.	1	2	3	4	5	6
6. I have very strong ties with my present job which would be very difficult to break.	1	2	3	4	5	6
7. Usually I feel detached from my job.	1	2	3	4	5	6
8. Most of my personal life goals are job-oriented.	1	2	3	4	5	6
9. I consider my job to be very central to my existence.	1	2	3	4	5	6
10. I like to be absorbed in my job most of the time.	1	2	3	4	5	6

Source: R.N. Kanungo, *Work Alienation* (New York: Praeger, 1982). Evaluated in J.L. Price and C.W. Mueller, *Handbook of Organizational Measurement* (Marshfield, MA: Pitman, 1986), pp. 174-77.

Scoring Key

To calculate your total, add up your scores from items 1, 3, 4, 5, 6, 8, 9, and 10. For items 2 and 7, reverse your score (6 becomes 1, 5 becomes 2, and so forth).

Analysis and Interpretation

This instrument taps job involvement--the degree to which you identify with your job, actively participate in it, and consider your performance important to your self-worth.

Your total will fall somewhere between 10 and 60. The higher your score, the more involved you are in your job. Studies conducted by the author found mean scores of 31.3. However, these scores are now quite dated. For general purposes, you might assume that scores above 40 indicate relatively high involvement; and scores below 25 as relatively low.

High job involvement is a two-edge sword. It suggests that you enjoy your job. But high involvement can make it hard for you to adjust if your job is eliminated. Additionally, the behaviors associated with high involvement can make it difficult for you to enjoy leisure time or pursue a balanced life. Obsessive emphasis on your job can undermine your personal relationships. If you score high on job involvement and are concerned that you're shortchanging your personal life, you should consider taking advantage of programs your employer might offer that could improve your work/life balance—for instance, flextime, telecommuting, on-site child care, or extended sabbaticals.

I.B.3: How Satisfied Am I With My Job?

Instrument

For the 20 items on this questionnaire, select your response from one of the following:

    1 = Very dissatisfied
    2 = Dissatisfied
    3 = I can't decide whether I am satisfied or not
    4 = Satisfied
    5 = Very satisfied

On my present job, this is how I feel about:

	1	2	3	4	5
1. Being able to keep busy all the time.	1	2	3	4	5
2. The chance to work alone on the job.	1	2	3	4	5
3. The chance to do different things from time to time.	1	2	3	4	5
4. The chance to be "somebody" in the community.	1	2	3	4	5
5. The way my boss handles his/her workers.	1	2	3	4	5
6. The competence of my supervisor in making decisions.	1	2	3	4	5
7. Being able to do things that don't go against my conscience.	1	2	3	4	5
8. The way my job provides for steady employment.	1	2	3	4	5
9. The chance to do things for other people.	1	2	3	4	5
10. The chance to tell people what to do.	1	2	3	4	5
11. The chance to do something that makes use of my abilities.	1	2	3	4	5
12. The way company policies are put into practice.	1	2	3	4	5
13. My pay and the amount of work I do.	1	2	3	4	5
14. The chances for advancement on this job.	1	2	3	4	5
15. The freedom to use my own judgment.	1	2	3	4	5
16. The chance to try my own methods of doing the job.	1	2	3	4	5
17. The working conditions.	1	2	3	4	5
18. The way my coworkers get along with each other.	1	2	3	4	5
19. The praise I get for doing a good job.	1	2	3	4	5
20. The feeling of accomplishment I get from my job.	1	2	3	4	5

Source: D.J. Weiss, R.V. Dawis, G.W. England, and L.H. Lofquist, *Manual for the Minnesota Satisfaction Questionnaire* (Minneapolis: University of Minnesota Industrial Relations Center, 1967). Evaluated in J.L. Price and C.W. Mueller, *Handbook of Organizational Measurement* (Marshfield, MA: Pitman, 1986), pp. 228-31.

Scoring Key

To score this instrument, add up your responses to all 20 items. Your total will be somewhere between 20 and 100.

Analysis and Interpretation

Job satisfaction is your general attitude about your job. High satisfaction tends to be related to lower levels of absenteeism and turnover. And, of course, high satisfaction is likely to spillover into raising your overall level of life satisfaction.

Studies using this instrument tend to find means in the 74 to 76 range. If you scored low, you might want to look at specific items in this questionnaire. Are there certain aspects of your job--supervision, pay, lack of advancement potential, coworkers, the work itself--that are causing problems? What, if anything, can be done to improve them? It may also be that your low satisfaction is due to *you* and not your job. That is, you may have a negative genetic predisposition toward life. So regardless of the job you're in, you may just tend to be unhappy.

I.B.4: What Are My Attitudes Toward Workplace Diversity?

Instrument

Listed below are 70 words that depict both positive and negative reactions to diversity. Circle all the words below that you frequently associate with workplace diversity.

Compassionate	Ethical	Anger	Unfair
Resentment	Wisdom	Insecurity	Progress
Unity	Bureaucratic	Proud	Justified
Stress	Fight	Cooperate	Happy
Support	Listen	Blame	Rivalry
Bad	Fear	Clashes	Confused
Discovery	Sensible	Frustration	Turnover
Stubbornness	Grateful	Unjustified	Harmony
Liability	Team-building	Participate	Asset
Innovation	Expensive	Hopeful	Understand
Useless	Rewarding	Sacrifice	Worthless
Unprofitable	Good	Withdrawal	Patronize
Fair	Pressure	Merit	Enthusiastic
Excited	Collaborate	Unfriendly	Profitable
Disorder	Immoral	Regulations	Useful
Resist	Unnatural	Proper	Disagree
Sleeplessness	Advancement	Enrichment	Apprehensive
Opportunity	Friendly		

Source: K. P. DeMeuse and T. J. Hostager, "Developing an Instrument for Measuring Attitudes Toward and Perceptions of Workplace Diversity: An Initial Report," *Human Resource Development Quarterly*, Spring 2001, pp. 33-51.

Scoring Key

Give yourself **+1** for each of the following words circled: *Compassionate, Ethical, Wisdom, Progress, Unity, Proud, Justified, Cooperate, Happy, Support, Listen, Discovery, Sensible, Graceful, Harmony, Team-Building, Participate, Asset, Innovation, Hopeful, Understand, Rewarding, Good, Fair, Merit, Enthusiastic, Excited, Collaborate, Profitable, Useful, Proper, Advancement, Enrichment, Opportunity, Friendly.*

Give yourself **–1** for each of the following words circled: *Anger, Unfair, Resentment, Insecurity, Bureaucratic, Stress, Fight, Blame, Rivalry, Bad, Fear, Clashes, Confused, Frustration, Turnover, Stubbornness, Unjustified, Liability, Expensive, Useless, Sacrifice, Worthless, Unprofitable, Withdrawal, Patronize, Pressure, Unfriendly, Disorder, Immoral, Regulations, Resist, Unnatural, Disagree, Sleeplessness, Apprehensive.*

Sum the pluses and minuses. Scores will range from +35 to –35.

Analysis and Interpretation

This instrument taps into five dimensions that represent the range of positive and negative reactions to workplace diversity. These are: emotional reactions, judgments, behavioral reactions, personal consequences, and organizational outcomes.

Your result will range from +35 to –35. The researchers categorized individuals by their total scores as follows:

+35 to +11. These are classified as diversity optimists.

+10 to –10. These are diversity realists.

-11 to –35. These are diversity pessimists.

For comparative purposes, the researchers tested this questionnaire on two groups of managers, two groups of employees, and a group of university students. Their scores were (all plus) 8.1, 13.6, 8.7, 9.7, and 5.1, respectively. None of the 40 managers who took the test were classified as pessimists; rather, half were optimists and half were realists. The 116 employees tested closely mirrored the managers, with 46 percent optimists and 49 percent realists. The university sample of 110 students was the least optimistic, with only 35 percent in that category.

If you fell into the pessimistic category, you're likely to have difficulty accepting the increasing diversity in today's workplace. You may want to read more on the benefits of diversity. Some relevant readings might include: T. H. Cox and S. Blake, "Managing Cultural Diversity: Implications for Organizational Competitiveness," *Academy of Management Executive*, vol. 5, 1991, pp. 45-56; J. P. Fernandez and M. Barr, *The Diversity Advantage* (San Francisco: New Lexington Press, 1993); and D. A. Thomas and R. J. Ely, "Making Differences Matter: A New Paradigm for Managing Diversity," *Harvard Business Review*, vol. 74, no. 5, 1996, pp. 79-90.

I.C.1: What Motivates Me?

Instrument

Indicate how important each of these points is in the job you would like to get. Use the following rating scale for your responses:

> 1 = Not important
> 2 = Slightly important
> 3 = Moderately important
> 4 = Very important
> 5 = Extremely important

	1	2	3	4	5
1. Cooperative relations with my co-workers.	1	2	3	4	5
2. Developing new skills and knowledge at work.	1	2	3	4	5
3. Good pay for my work.	1	2	3	4	5
4. Being accepted by others.	1	2	3	4	5
5. Opportunity for independent thought and action.	1	2	3	4	5
6. Frequent raises in pay.	1	2	3	4	5
7. Opportunity to develop close friendships at work.	1	2	3	4	5
8. A sense of self-esteem.	1	2	3	4	5
9. A complete fringe-benefit program.	1	2	3	4	5
10. Openness and honesty with my co-workers.	1	2	3	4	5
11. Opportunities for personal growth and development.	1	2	3	4	5
12. A sense of security from bodily harm.	1	2	3	4	5

Source: Adapted with permission of The Free Press, from *Existence, Relatedness, and Growth: Human Needs in Organizational Settings*, by C.P. Alderfer. Copyright c 1972 by The Free Press.

Scoring Key

To calculate your score, add the items in each need set as follows:

> Items 2, 5, 8, 11 = Growth needs
> Items 1, 4, 7, 10 = Relatedness needs
> Items 3, 6, 9, 12 = Existence needs

Analysis and Interpretation

This instrument taps the three needs of growth, relatedness, and existence. It is based on what is known as ERG Theory.

If you considered all four items within a need category to be extremely important, you would obtain the maximum total of twenty points.

College students typically rate growth needs highest. However, you may currently have little income and consider existence needs as most important. For instance, one student of mine scored 20, 10, and 15 for growth, relatedness, and existence needs, respectively. This should be interpreted to mean that her relatedness needs are already substantially satisfied. Her growth needs, on the other hand, are substantially unsatisfied.

Note that a low score may imply that a need is unimportant to you or that it is substantially satisfied. The implication, however, is that *everyone* has these needs. So a low score is usually taken to mean that this need is substantially satisfied.

I.C.2: What Are My Dominant Needs?

Instrument

This test contains 20 statements that may describe you and the types of things you may like to do. For each statement, indicate your agreement or disagreement using the following scale:

        1 = Strongly disagree
        2 = Disagree
        3 = Neither agree nor disagree
        4 = Agree
        5 = Strongly agree

1. I try to perform my best at work.	1	2	3	4	5
2. I spent a lot of time talking to other people.	1	2	3	4	5
3. I would like a career where I have very little supervision.	1	2	3	4	5
4. I would enjoy being in charge of a project.	1	2	3	4	5
5. I am a hard worker.	1	2	3	4	5
6. I am a "people" person.	1	2	3	4	5
7. I would like a job where I can plan my work schedule myself.	1	2	3	4	5
8. I would rather receive orders than give them.	1	2	3	4	5
9. It is important to me to do the best job possible.	1	2	3	4	5
10. When I have a choice, I try to work in a group instead of by myself.	1	2	3	4	5
11. I would like to be my own boss.	1	2	3	4	5
12. I seek an active role in the leadership of a group.	1	2	3	4	5
13. I push myself to be "all that I can be."	1	2	3	4	5
14. I prefer to do my work and let others do theirs.	1	2	3	4	5
15. I like to work at my own pace on job tasks.	1	2	3	4	5
16. I find myself organizing and directing the activities of others.	1	2	3	4	5
17. I try very hard to improve on my past performance at work.	1	2	3	4	5
18. I try my best to work alone on a work assignment.	1	2	3	4	5
19. In my work projects, I try to be my own boss.	1	2	3	4	5
20. I strive to be "in command" when I am working in a group.	1	2	3	4	5

Source: T. M. Heckert, G. Cuneio, A. P. Hannah, P. J. Adams, H. E. Droste, M. A. Mueller, H. A. Wallis, C. M. Griffin, and L. L. Roberts, "Creation of a New Needs Assessment Questionnaire," *Journal of Social Behavior and Personality*, March 2000, pp. 121-36.

Scoring Key

Add up items 1, 5, 9, 13 and 17. These represent the achievement score. The affiliation score is made up of items 1, 6, 10, 14, and 18 (reverse-score 14 and 18). The autonomy score is items 3, 7, 11, 15, and 19. The power score is items 4 (reverse score), 8, 12, 16, and 20. Scores will range for each from 5-25.

Analysis and Interpretation

This instrument was designed to deal with flaws in previous attempts to measure four social needs: achievement, affiliation, autonomy, and power. These are defined as follows:

Achievement – The desire to excel and to improve on past performance.

Affiliation – The desire to interact socially and to be accepted by others.

Autonomy – The desire to be self-directed.

Power – The desire to influence and direct others.

Your score on each will vary between 5 and 25. The higher a score, the more dominant that need is for you. For comparative purposes, the researchers used this test with approximately 350 college graduates who averaged 28 years of age. Their average scores were 22.6 for achievement; 16.1 for affiliation; 20.0 for autonomy; and 17.7 for power.

I.C.3: What Rewards Do I Value Most?

Instrument

This test contains ten work-related rewards. For each, identify the response that best describes the value that a particular reward has for you personally. Use the following scale to express your feelings:

$$1 = \text{No value at all}$$
$$2 = \text{Slight value}$$
$$3 = \text{Moderate value}$$
$$4 = \text{Great value}$$
$$5 = \text{Extremely great value}$$

1. Good pay	1	2	3	4	5
2. Prestigious title	1	2	3	4	5
3. Vacation time	1	2	3	4	5
4. Job security	1	2	3	4	5
5. Recognition	1	2	3	4	5
6. Interesting work	1	2	3	4	5
7. Pleasant conditions	1	2	3	4	5
8. Chances to advance	1	2	3	4	5
9. Flexible schedule	1	2	3	4	5
10. Friendly coworkers	1	2	3	4	5

Source: J. Greenberg and R.A. Baron, *Behavior in Organizations*, 6th ed. (Upper Saddle River, NJ: Prentice Hall, 1997), p. 173.

Scoring Key

To assess your responses, prioritize them into groups. Put all the ones you gave a "5" together. Do the same for your other responses.

Analysis and Interpretation

What motivates *you* doesn't necessarily motivate *me*. So employers that want to maximize employee motivation should determine what rewards each employee individually values. This instrument can help you to understand what work-related rewards have the greatest value to you.

The rewards that you identified as having "great value" or "extremely great value" are the ones that you most desire and which your employer should emphasize *with you*.

Compare the rewards that your employer offers with your scores. The greater the disparity, the more you might want to consider looking for opportunities at another organization with a reward structure that better matches your preferences.

I.C.4: What's My View on the Nature of People?

Instrument
Indicate your agreement or disagreement with each of the eight statements using the following scale:

        1 = Strongly disagree
        2 = Disagree
        3 = Undecided
        4 = Agree
        5 = Strongly agree

1. The average human being prefers to be directed, wishes to avoid responsibility, and has relatively little ambition.   1   2   3   4   5

2. Most people can acquire leadership skills regardless of their particular inborn traits and abilities.   1   2   3   4   5

3. The use of rewards (for example, pay and promotion) and punishment (for example, failure to promote) is the best way to get subordinates to do their work.   1   2   3   4   5

4. In a work situation, if the subordinate can influence you, you lose some influence over them.   1   2   3   4   5

5. A good leader gives detailed and complete instructions to subordinates rather than giving them merely general directions and depending on their initiative to work out the details.   1   2   3   4   5

6. Individual goal setting offers advantages that cannot be obtained by group goal setting, because groups do not set high goals.   1   2   3   4   5

7. A superior should give subordinates only the information necessary for them to do their immediate tasks.   1   2   3   4   5

8. The superior's influence over subordinates in an organization is primarily economic.   1   2   3   4   5

Source: Adapted from M. Haire, E. Ghiselli, and L. Porter, *Managerial Thinking: An International Study*, Appendix A. Copyright c 1966 by John Wiley & Sons, Inc. Reprinted with permission.

Scoring Key
To calculate your Theory X-Theory Y orientation, add up your scores for the eight statements.

Analysis and Interpretation
This instrument was designed to tap your view of human nature. It is based on Douglas McGregor's Theory X and Theory Y.

McGregor proposed that individuals tend to view others in either negative or positive terms. The negative stereotype, which he called Theory X, sees human beings as primarily lazy and disinterested in working. In contrast, Theory Y views them as responsible and hard working under the right conditions.

Your total score will range between 8 and 40. A score of 32 or more indicates a tendency to accept Theory X assumptions. A score of 15 or less indicates a tendency to accept Theory Y assumptions. A score between 16 and 31 indicates flexibility in your perception of others.

Theory X and Theory Y are often misunderstood as being styles of management. They aren't. They're beliefs about human nature. However, it's a small and logical step to conclude that people who hold Theory X assumptions tend to manage more autocratically; while those holding Theory Y assumptions tend to be more democratic managers.

Your score can give you insights into your inherent view of people and how best to manage them. However, you are not locked into a particular management or leadership style based on your view of human nature. Your views reflect a tendency, not a mandate. But your score may help you better understand why, when filling a leadership role in groups, you tend to be autocratic or supportive and trusting.

I.C.5: What Are My Course Performance Goals?

Instrument
Using the following scale, select the answer for each of the 12 statements that best expresses why you study for a course.

    1 = Never
    2 = Rarely
    3 = Sometimes
    4 = Often
    5 = Always

I study because:

1. I want to be praised by my professors and parents.	1	2	3	4	5
1. I want to be noticed by my friends.	1	2	3	4	5
2. I don't want my classmates to make fun of me.	1	2	3	4	5
3. I don't want to be disliked by a professor.	1	2	3	4	5
4. I want people to see how smart I am.	1	2	3	4	5
5. I wish to get better grades than my peers.	1	2	3	4	5
6. I want to get good grades.	1	2	3	4	5
7. I want to be proud of getting good grades.	1	2	3	4	5
8. I don't want to fail final exams.	1	2	3	4	5
9. I wish to be admitted to graduate school.	1	2	3	4	5
10. I want to get a good job in the future.	1	2	3	4	5
11. I want to attain status in the future.	1	2	3	4	5

Source: T. Hayamizu and B. Weiner, "A Test of Dweck's Model of Achievement Goals as Related to Perceptions of Ability," *Journal of Experimental Education*, vol. 59, 1991, pp. 226-34. Modified per C. Dupeyrat and E. V. Smith Jr., "Toward Establishing a Unified Metric for Performance and Learning Goal Orientations," *Journal of Applied Measurement*, vol. 2, no. 4, 2001, pp. 312-36.

Scoring Key
Total up the number of 4 and 5 responses. This will be between zero and 12.

Analysis and Interpretation
What drives you to study? What goals are you trying to achieve? This questionnaire measures goal orientation as related to your course work.

There are no "right" goals. But having clear goals can help you better understand your studying behavior. If you had no responses in the 4 or 5 categories, your course performance is likely to suffer because you have no strong reasons for studying. This suggests a need for you to reassess your goals and consider what you want from your course work. If you had a number of responses in the 4 or 5 categories, you appear to have specific goals that will motivate you to study and achieve high performance.

I.C.6: How Confident Am I in My Abilities to Succeed?

Instrument
To what extent does each of these 17 statements describe you? Indicate your level of agreement by using the following scale:

> 1 = Strongly Disagree
> 2 = Disagree
> 3 = Neutral
> 4 = Agree
> 5 = Strongly Agree

1. When I make plans, I am certain I can make them work. 1	2	3	4	5
2. One of my problems is that I cannot get down to work when I should 1	2	3	4	5
3. If I can't do a job the first time, I keep trying until I can. 1	2	3	4	5
4. When I set important goals for myself, I rarely achieve them. 1	2	3	4	5
5. I give up on things before completing them. 1	2	3	4	5
6. I avoid facing difficulties. 1	2	3	4	5
7. If something looks too complicated, I will not even bother to try it. 1	2	3	4	5
8. When I have something unpleasant to do, I stick to it until I finish it. 1	2	3	4	5
9. When I decide to do something, I go right to work on it. 1	2	3	4	5
10. When trying to learn something new, I soon give up if I am not initially successful. 1	2	3	4	5
11. When unexpected problems occur, I don't handle them well. 1	2	3	4	5
12. I avoid trying to learn new things when they look too difficult for me. 1	2	3	4	5
13. Failure just makes me try harder. 1	2	3	4	5
14. I feel insecure about my ability to do things. 1	2	3	4	5
15. I am a self-reliant person. 1	2	3	4	5
16. I give up easily. 1	2	3	4	5
17. I do not seem capable of dealing with most problems that come up in life. 1	2	3	4	5

Source: M. Sherer, J. E. Maddux, B. Mercandante, S. Prentice-Dunn, B. Jacobs, and R. W. Rogers, "The Self-Efficacy Scale: Construction and Validation," *Psychological Reports*, vol. 51, 1982, pp. 663-71.

Scoring Key
Add up the scores for items 2, 4, 5, 6, 7, 10, 11, 12, 14, 16, and 17. For the other six items, reverse the scoring: Strongly agree becomes 1, agree becomes 2, and so on.

Analysis and Interpretation

This test is designed to assess your self-efficacy. This is defined as your belief that you're capable of successfully performing a task. Your score will range between 17 and 85. The higher your score, the higher your level of self-efficacy. While no exact cut-off scores are available, scores of 60 or higher generally suggest strong self-efficacy. You tend to be confident when facing new tasks or challenges. Scores below 45 indicate that you could use more self-confidence and that you may often be your own worst enemy. In difficult situations, people with low self-efficacy are more likely to lessen their effort or just give up, while those with high self-efficacy are more likely to try harder to master the challenge.

I.C.7: What's My Attitude Toward Achievement?

Instrument

Using the following scale, select the answer that best expresses your opinion on each of the 20 questions. Try to minimize the use of the "In between or don't know" answer.

> 1 = I disagree very much
> 2 = I disagree on the whole
> 3 = I disagree a little
> 4 = In between or don't know
> 5 = I agree a little
> 6 = I agree on the whole
> 7 = I agree very much

1. People who are very successful deserve all the rewards
    they get for their achievements.   1 2 3 4 5 6 7
2. It's good to see very successful people fail occasionally.   1 2 3 4 5 6 7
3. Very successful people often get too big for their boots.   1 2 3 4 5 6 7
4. People who are very successful in what they do are
    usually friendly and helpful to others.   1 2 3 4 5 6 7
5. At school it's probably better for students to be near
    the middle of the class than the very top student.   1 2 3 4 5 6 7
6. People shouldn't criticize or knock the very successful.   1 2 3 4 5 6 7
7. Very successful people who fall from the top usually
    deserve their fall from grace.   1 2 3 4 5 6 7
8. Those who are very successful ought to come down
    off their pedestals and be like other people.   1 2 3 4 5 6 7
9. The very successful person should receive public
    recognition for his/her accomplishments.   1 2 3 4 5 6 7
10. People who are very successful should be cut down
    to size.   1 2 3 4 5 6 7
11. One should always respect the person at the top.   1 2 3 4 5 6 7
12. One ought to be sympathetic to very successful
    people when they experience failure and fall from
    their very high positions.   1 2 3 4 5 6 7
13. Very successful people sometimes need to be brought
    back a peg or two, even if they have done nothing
    wrong.   1 2 3 4 5 6 7
14. Society needs a lot of very high achievers.   1 2 3 4 5 6 7
15. People who always do a lot better than others need to
    learn what it's like to fail.   1 2 3 4 5 6 7
16. People who are right at the top usually deserve their
    high position.   1 2 3 4 5 6 7
17. It's very important for society to support and
    encourage people who are very successful.   1 2 3 4 5 6 7
18. People who are very successful get too full of their
    own importance.   1 2 3 4 5 6 7

19. Very successful people usually succeed at the
    expense of other people.   1   2   3   4   5   6   7

20. Very successful people who are at the top of their
    field are usually fun to be with.   1   2   3   4   5   6   7

Source: Adapted from N. T. Feather, "Attitudes Toward the High Achiever: The Fall of the Tall Poppy," *Australian Journal of Psychology*, Vol. 41, 1989, pp. 239-67.

Scoring Key

To calculate your first score, add your responses to the following ten items: 2, 3, 5, 7, 8, 10, 13, 15, 18, and 19. For your second score, add your responses to the remaining ten items.

Analysis and Interpretation

This instrument was developed to measure attitudes toward the success and achievement of others. Emphasis is on the display of conspicuous success.

    This questionnaire generates two scores, both of which will range between 10 and 70. The higher your first score, the more you favor seeing very successful people fall. The higher your second score, the more you favor the reward of the very successful.

    This instrument was developed in Australia. And although Australians value achievement, they are very ambivalent about its public expression. They tend to enjoy seeing the conspicuously successful fall from grace. In a sample of Australian adults, the average fall score was 38, and the average reward score was 45.

    The results from this instrument can help you better understand why you react the way you do to others' success. It can also help you assess how important achievement is to your life goals.

I.C.8: What's My Job's Motivating Potential?

Instrument

Describe your present job (or a previous paid or unpaid job you've had) using the following questionnaire. Choose the number (1-7) that best describes the job. You must use a whole number.

1. How much *variety* is there in your job? That is, to what extent does the job require you to do many different things at work, using a variety of your skills and talents?

1	2	3	4	5	6	7

Very little; the job requires me to do the same routine things over and over again.

Moderate variety.

Very much; the job requires me to do many different things, using a number of different skills and talents.

2. To what extent does your job involve doing a "*whole:*" and *identifiable piece of work*? That is, is the job a complete piece of work that has an obvious beginning and end, or is it only a small part of the overall piece of work, which is finished by other people or by machines?

1	2	3	4	5	6	7

My job is only a tiny part of the overall piece of work; the results of my activities cannot be seen in the final product or service.

My job is a moderate-sized "chunk" of the overall piece of work; my own contribution can seen in the final outcome.

My job involves doing the whole piece of work, from start to finish; the results of my activities are easily seen in the final product or service.

3. In general, *how significant or important* is your job? That is, are the results of your work likely to significantly affect the lives or well-being of other people?

1	2	3	4	5	6	7

Not very significant; the outcomes of my work are not likely to have important effects on other people.

Moderately significant.

Highly significant; the outcomes of my work can affect other people in very important ways.

4. How much *autonomy* is there in your job? That is, to what extent does your job permit you to decide *on your own* how to go about doing the work?

1	2	3	4	5	6	7

Very little; the job gives me almost no personal "say" about how and when the work is done.

Moderate autonomy; many things are standardized and not under my control, but I can make some decisions about the work.

Very much; the job gives me almost complete responsibility for deciding how and when the work is done.

5. To what extent does doing *the job itself* provide you with information about your work performance? That is, does the actual *work itself* provide clues about how well you are doing-- aside from any feedback co-workers or supervisors may provide?

1	2	3	4	5	6	7
Very little; the job itself is set up so that I could work forever without finding out how well I am doing.			Moderately; sometimes doing the job provides feedback to me; some-times it does not.		Very much; the job is set up so that I get almost constant feedback as I work about how well I am doing.	

Source: Adapted from J.R. Hackman and G.R. Oldham, *Work Redesign* (Reading, MA: Addison-Wesley, 1980), pp. 277-79.

Scoring Key

To calculate your score, insert your responses from the questionnaire (the numbers 1 through 7) into the following formula:

$$MPS = \left(\frac{\text{Skill variety (Ques. \# 1)} + \text{Task identity (\#2)} + \text{Task significance (\#3)}}{3}\right) \times \text{Autonomy (\#4)} \times \text{Feedback (\#5)}$$

Analysis and Interpretation

This questionnaire allows you to calculate your Motivating Potential Score (MPS) from the Job Characteristics Model. The MPS represents a summary score indicating how motivating you find the jobs you're describing.

Studies indicate that jobs that score high on all five of these dimensions are likely to stimulate motivation, high performance, and high satisfaction for job incumbents. Additionally, high scores are associated with reduced absenteeism and turnover.

The higher your score, the higher your job's motivating potential. MPS scores can range from 1 to 343, with the average score being 128.

I.C.9: Do I Want an Enriched Job?

Instrument
Listed to the right are 12 pairs of jobs shown on two screens (Job A is on the upper screen and Job B on the lower screen). For each pair, indicate which job you would prefer—Job A or Job B. Assume that everything else about the jobs is the same. Use the following rating scale for your responses, and try to minimize your use of the "neutral" selection:

<blockquote>

1 = Strongly prefer A
2 = Prefer A
3 = Slightly prefer A
4 = Neutral
5 = Slightly prefer B
6 = Prefer B
7 = Strongly prefer B
</blockquote>

Column A		Column B
1. A job that offers little or no challenge.	1 2 3 4 5 6 7	A job that requires you to be completely isolated from coworkers.
2. A job that pays very well.	1 2 3 4 5 6 7	A job that allows considerable opportunity to be creative and innovative.
3. A job that often requires you to make important decisions.	1 2 3 4 5 6 7	A job in which there are many pleasant people to work with.
4. A job with little security in a somewhat unstable organization.	1 2 3 4 5 6 7	A job in which you have little or no opportunity to participate in decisions which affect your work.
5. A job in which greater responsibility is given to those who do the best work.	1 2 3 4 5 6 7	A job in which great responsibility is given to loyal employees who have the most seniority.
6. A job with a supervisor who sometimes is highly critical.	1 2 3 4 5 6 7	A job that does not require you to use much of your talent.
7. A very routine job.	1 2 3 4 5 6 7	A job where your co-workers are not very friendly.

8. A job with a supervisor who respects you and treats you fairly.	1	2	3	4	5	6	7	A job that provides constant opportunities for you to learn new and interesting things.
9. A job that gives you a real chance to develop yourself personally.	1	2	3	4	5	6	7	A job with excellent vacations and fringe benefits.
10. A job where there is a real chance you could be laid off.	1	2	3	4	5	6	7	A job with very little chance to do challenging work.
11. A job with little freedom and independence to do your work in the way you think best.	1	2	3	4	5	6	7	A job with poor working conditions.
12. A job with very satisfying teamwork.	1	2	3	4	5	6	7	A job that allows you to use your skills and abilities to the fullest extent.

Source: Adapted from J.R. Hackman and G.R. Oldham (1974). The Job Diagnostic Survey: An instrument for the Diagnosis of Jobs and the Evaluation of Job Redesign Projects. Technical Report No. 4. New Haven, Conn.: Yale University, Department of Administrative Sciences. With permission.

Scoring Key
To calculate your growth need strength score, average the 12 items as follows:
> #1, #2, #7, #8, #11, #12 (direct scoring)
> #3, #4, #5, #6, #9, #10 (reverse scoring)

Analysis and Interpretation
This instrument is designed to assess the degree to which you desire complex, challenging work. A high need for growth suggests that you are more likely to experience the desired psychological states in the Job Characteristics Model when you have an enriched job.

This 12-item instrument taps the degree to which you have a strong versus weak desire to obtain growth satisfaction from your work.

Average scores for typical respondents are close to the midpoint of 4.0. Research indicates that if you score high on this measure, you will respond positively to an enriched job. (See Exercise #20). Conversely, if you score low, you will tend *not* to find enriched jobs satisfying or motivating.

I.D.1: Am I a Procrastinator?

Instrument

The following lists a variety of thoughts that sometimes pop into people's heads. Read each thought and indicate how frequently, if at all, you think the thought has occurred to you during the past two weeks. Use the following rating scale:

  0 = Not at all
  1 = Sometimes
  2 = Moderately often
  3 = Often
  4 = All the time

1. Why can't I do what I *should* be doing.	0	1	2	3	4
2. I need to start earlier.	0	1	2	3	4
3. I should be more responsible.	0	1	2	3	4
4. No matter how much I try, I still put things off.	0	1	2	3	4
5. Why can't I just get started.	0	1	2	3	4
6. I know I'm behind but I can catch up.	0	1	2	3	4
7. I'm letting myself down.	0	1	2	3	4
8. This is not how I want to be.	0	1	2	3	4
8. It would be great if everything in my life were done on time.	0	1	2	3	4
10. I'm such a procrastinator, I'll never reach my goals.	0	1	2	3	4
11. I need deadlines to get me going.	0	1	2	3	4
12. Why can't I finish things that I start.	0	1	2	3	4
13. Why didn't I start earlier.	0	1	2	3	4

Source: Adapted from M. Stainton, C. H. Lay, and G. L. Flett, "Trait Procrastinators and Behavior/Trait-Specific Cognitions," *Journal of Social Behavior and Personality*, vol. 15, no. 5, 2000, pp. 297-312. Reprinted with permission.

Scoring Key

Add up individual responses for the 13 items.

Analysis and Interpretation

Procrastination is a tendency to postpone, delay, or avoid performing tasks or making decisions. In some situations, procrastination can be positive. For instance, if you lack sufficient information to make an informed decision, if other pressing matters with higher priorities demand attention, or if the consequences of a decision are so weighty that more deliberation is needed, procrastination is likely to reduce the chances of making a bad decision. However, chronic procrastination can lead to lost opportunities, regrets, and other negative outcomes.

Your score will range somewhere between 0 and 52. The higher your score, the more you're prone to procrastinate. Scores of 13 or less suggest you don't delay decisions or life activities. Scores of 35 or higher, on the other hand, indicate you may be prone to postpone doing things and experience frustrations over actions not taken.

For many people, procrastination consistently hinders them from taking actions and changing things in their lives, but low scores on this test also may indicate problems. Low procrastinators often act prematurely and later regret their actions.

I.D.2: How Do My Ethics Rate?

Instrument
Indicate your level of agreement with these 15 statements using the following scale:

        1 = Strongly disagree
        2 = Disagree
        3 = Neither agree or disagree
        4 = Agree
        5 = Strongly agree

1. The only moral of business is making money.   1   2   3   4   5
2. A person who is doing well in business does not have to worry about moral problems.   1   2   3   4   5
3. Act according to the law, and you can't go wrong morally.   1   2   3   4   5
4. Ethics in business is basically an adjustment between expectations and the ways people behave.   1   2   3   4   5
5. Business decisions involve a realistic economic attitude and not a moral philosophy.   1   2   3   4   5
6. "Business ethics" is a concept for public relations only.   1   2   3   4   5
7. Competitiveness and profitability are important values.   1   2   3   4   5
8. Conditions of a free economy will best serve the needs of society. Limiting competition can only hurt society and actually violates basic natural laws.   1   2   3   4   5
9. As a consumer, when making an auto insurance claim, I try to get as much as possible regardless of the extent of the damage.   1   2   3   4   5
10. While shopping at the supermarket, it is appropriate to switch price tags on packages.   1   2   3   4   5
11. As an employee, I can take home office supplies; it doesn't hurt anyone.   1   2   3   4   5
12. I view sick days as vacation days that I deserve.   1   2   3   4   5
13. Employees' wages should be determined according to the laws of supply and demand.   1   2   3   4   5
14. The business world has its own rules.   1   2   3   4   5
15. A good businessperson is a successful businessperson.   1   2   3   4   5

Source: Adapted from A. Reichel and Y. Neumann, *Journal of Instructional Psychology*, March 1988, pp. 25-53. With permission of the authors.

Analysis and Interpretation

No decision is completely value-free. It undoubtedly will have some ethical dimensions. This instrument presents philosophical positions and practical situations. Rather than specify "right" answers, this instrument works best when you compare your answers to those of others. With that in mind, here are mean responses from a group of 243 management students. How did your responses compare?

1. 3.09	6. 2.88	11. 1.58
2. 1.88	7. 3.62	12. 2.31
3. 2.54	8. 3.79	13. 3.36
4. 3.41	9. 3.44	14. 3.79
5. 3.88	10. 1.33	15. 3.38

Do you tend to be more or less ethical than the student norms presented above? On which items did you differ most? Your answers to these questions can provide insights into how well your ethical standards match other people with whom you will be working in the future. Large discrepancies might be a warning that others don't hold the same ethical values that you do.

I.E.1: What's My Emotional Intelligence Score?

Instrument
Indicate your level of agreement with these ten statements using the following scale:

        1 = Strongly disagree
        2 = Disagree
        3 = Neither agree or disagree
        4 = Agree
        5 = Strongly agree

1. I am usually aware—from moment to moment—of my feelings as they change.   1 2 3 4 5
2. I act before I think.   1 2 3 4 5
3. When I want something, I want it NOW!   1 2 3 4 5
4. I bounce back quickly from life's setbacks.   1 2 3 4 5
5. I can pick up subtle social cues that indicate others' needs or wants.   1 2 3 4 5
6. I'm very good at handling myself in social situations.   1 2 3 4 5
7. I'm persistent in going after the things I want.   1 2 3 4 5
8. When people share their problems with me, I'm good at putting myself in their shoes.   1 2 3 4 5
9. When I'm in a bad mood, I make a strong effort to get out of it.   1 2 3 4 5
9. I can find common ground and build rapport with people from all walks of life.   1 2 3 4 5

Source: Based on D. Goleman, *Emotional Intelligence: Why It Can Matter More Than IQ* (New York: Bantam Book, 1995).

Scoring Key
To calculate your EI score, add up your responses to the ten items; however, reverse your scores for items 2 and 3.

Analysis and Interpretation
Emotional intelligence (EI) is an assortment of skills and competencies that have shown to influence a person's ability to succeed in coping with environmental demands and pressures. People with high EI have the ability to accurately perceive, evaluate, express, and regulate emotions and feelings.

This questionnaire taps the five basic dimensions in EI: self-awareness (items 1 and 9), self-management (2, 4), self-motivation (3,7), empathy (5,8), and social skills (6,10).

Your score will fall between 10 and 50. While no definite cutoff scores are available, scores of 40 or higher indicate a high EI. Scores of 20 or less suggest a relatively low EI.

EI may be most predictive of performance in jobs such as sales or management where success is as dependent on interpersonal skills as technical ability. EI should also be relevant in selecting members to teams. People with low EI are likely to have difficulty managing others, making effective sales presentations, and working on teams.

Can EI be learned? A large part of an individual's EI is genetically based. However, you can improve on your EI. See, for instance, J. Segal, *Raising Your Emotional Intelligence* (Holt, 1997) and A. Simmons and J.C. Simmons, *Measuring Emotional Intelligence: The Groundbreaking Guide to Applying the Principles of Emotional Intelligence* (Summit, 1998).

I.E.2: What Time of Day Am I Most Productive?

Instrument
Indicate the response for each item that best describes you.

1. Considering only your own "feeling best" rhythm, at what time would you get up if you were entirely free to plan your day?
        a. 5:00-6:30 a.m.
        b. 6:30-7:45 a.m.
        c. 7:45-9:45 a.m.
        d. 9:45-11:00 a.m.
        e. 11:00 a.m.-12:00 (noon)

2. Considering only your "feeling best" rhythm, at what time would you go to bed if you were entirely free to plan your evening?
        a. 8:00-9:00 p.m.
        b. 9:00-10:15 p.m.
        c. 10:15 p.m.-12:30 a.m.
        d. 12:30-1:45 a.m.
        e. 1:45-3:00 a.m.

3. Assuming normal circumstances, how easy do you find getting up in the morning?
        a. Not at all easy
        b. Slightly easy
        c. Fairly easy
        d. Very easy

4. How alert do you feel during the first half hour after you wake up in the morning?
        a. Not at all alert
        b. Slightly alert
        c. Fairly alert
        d. Very alert

5. During the first half hour after awakening in the morning, how tired do you feel?
        a. Very tired
        b. Fairly tired
        c. Fairly refreshed
        d. Very refreshed

6. You have decided to engage in some physical exercise. A friend suggests that you do this one hour twice a week and the best time for him is 7:00-8:00 a.m. Bearing in mind nothing else but your own "feeling best" rhythm, how do you think you would perform?
        a. Would be in good form
        b. Would be in reasonable form
        c. Would find it difficult
        d. Would find it very difficult

7. At what time in the evening do you feel tired and, as a result, in need of sleep?
        a. 8:00-9:00 p.m.
        b. 9:00-10:15 p.m.
        c. 10:15 p.m.-12:30 a.m.
        d. 12:30-1:45 a.m.
        e. 1:45-3:00 a.m.

8. You wish to be at your peak performance for a test which you know is going to be mentally exhausting and will last for two hours. You are entirely free to plan your day, and considering only your own "feeling best" rhythm, which ONE of the four testing times would you choose?
        a. 8:00-10:00 a.m.
        b. 11:00 a.m.-1:00 p.m.
        c. 3:00-5:00 p.m.
        d. 7:00-9:00 p.m.

9. One hears about "morning" and "evening" types of people. Which ONE of these types do you consider yourself to be?
        a. Definitely a morning type
        b. More a morning than an evening type
        c. More an evening than a morning type
        d. Definitely an evening type

10. When would you prefer to rise (provided you have a full day's work--8 hours) if you were totally free to arrange your time?
        a. Before 6:30 a.m.
        b. 6:30-7:30 a.m.
        c. 7:30-8:30 a.m.
        d. 8:30 a.m. or later

11. If you always had to rise at 6:00 a.m., what do you think it would be like?
        a. Very difficult and unpleasant
        b. Rather difficult and unpleasant
        c. A little unpleasant but no great problem
        d. Easy and not unpleasant

12. How long a time does it usually take you before you "recover your senses" in the morning after rising from a night's sleep?
    a. 0-10 minutes
    b. 11-20 minutes
    c. 21-40 minutes
    d. More than 40 minutes

13. Please indicate the extent you are a morning or evening *active* individual.
    a. Pronounced morning active (morning alert and evening tired)
    b. To some extent, morning active
    c. To some extent, evening active
    d. Pronounced evening active (morning tired and evening alert)

Source: C.S. Smith, C. Reilly, and K. Midkiff, "Evaluation of Three Circadian Rhythm Questionnaires With Suggestions for an Improved Measure of Morningness," *Journal of Applied Psychology*, October 1989, p. 734.

Scoring Key
To calculate your score, add up the points allocated to the responses given.
  For items 1, 2, and 7: give 5 points for a; 4 points for b; down to 1 point for e.
  For items 3, 4, 5, and 11: give 1 point for a; 2 points for b; down to 4 points for d.
  For items 6, 8, 9, 10, 12, and 13: give 4 points for a; 3 points for b; down to 1 point for d.

Analysis and Interpretation
People differ in terms of when they are most alert and productive. This questionnaire taps your cycle to see whether you're more of a morning or evening person.

Score totals can range from 13 to 55. Scores of 22 and less indicate evening types; scores of 23-43 indicate intermediate types; and scores of 44 and above indicate morning types.

People have different cycles. Some of us do our best work early in the day, while others are most effective in the evenings. You should know your personal cycle so you can organize your work accordingly. Don't fight your natural rhythms. If you don't already do this, you should adjust your activities so your most important and challenging activities are undertaken when your cycle is high and put off the more mundane and routine activities to when your cycle is low.

I.E.3: How Good Am I at Personal Planning?

Instrument
Indicate how much you agree or disagree with each of the six statements as they relate to your school and personal life. Use the following scale to record your answers:

        1 = Strongly disagree
        2 = Disagree
        3 = Neither agree or disagree
        4 = Agree
        5 = Strongly agree

1. I am proactive rather than reactive.	1	2	3	4	5
2. I set aside enough time and resources to study and complete projects.	1	2	3	4	5
3. I am able to budget money to buy the things I really want without going broke.	1	2	3	4	5
4. I have thought through what I want to do in school.	1	2	3	4	5
5. I have a plan for completing my major.	1	2	3	4	5
6. My goals for the future are realistic.	1	2	3	4	5

Source: R.E. Quinn, S.R. Faerman, M.P. Thompson, and M.R. McGrath, *Becoming a Master Manager: A Competency Framework* (New York: Wiley, 1990), pp. 33-34.

Analysis and Interpretation
Successful people have goals and establish plans to help them achieve those goals. This exercise is designed to get you to think about goal setting as it relates to your school and personal life.

The authors of this instrument suggest that any item you didn't agree with indicates you need to gain a better understanding of the importance of goal-setting and what is involved in the process.

If your performance on this instrument was less than you desire, you should consider practicing skills related to goal-setting and time management. Toward that end, you might want to read one or more of the following books: D.K. Smith, *Make Success Measurable! A Mindbook-Workbook for Setting Goals and Taking Action* (Wiley, 1999); G.R. Blair, *Goal Setting 101: How to Set and Achieve a Goal!* (The Goals Guy, 2000); or M. Leboeuf, *Working Smart: How to Accomplish More in Half the Time* (Warner, 1993).

I.E.4: Am I Likely to Become An Entrepreneur?

Instrument
Respond to each of the 17 statements using the following rating scale:

    1 = Strongly disagree
    2 = Moderately disagree
    3 = Slightly disagree
    4 = Neither agree or disagree
    5 = Slightly agree
    6 = Moderately agree
    7 = Strongly agree

1. I am constantly on the lookout for new ways to improve my life.   1 2 3 4 5 6 7
2. I feel driven to make a difference in my community, and maybe the world.   1 2 3 4 5 6 7
3. I tend to let others take the initiative to start new projects.   1 2 3 4 5 6 7
4. Wherever I have been, I have been a powerful force for constructive change.   1 2 3 4 5 6 7
5. I enjoy facing and overcoming obstacles to my ideas.   1 2 3 4 5 6 7
6. Nothing is more exciting than seeing my ideas turn into reality.   1 2 3 4 5 6 7
7. If I see something I don't like, I fix it.   1 2 3 4 5 6 7
8. No matter what the odds, if I believe in something I will make it happen.   1 2 3 4 5 6 7
9. I love being a champion for my ideas, even against others' opposition.   1 2 3 4 5 6 7
10. I excel at identifying opportunities.   1 2 3 4 5 6 7
11. I am always looking for better ways to do things.   1 2 3 4 5 6 7
12. If I believe in an idea, no obstacle will prevent me from making it happen.   1 2 3 4 5 6 7
13. I love to challenge the status quo.   1 2 3 4 5 6 7
14. When I have a problem, I tackle it head-on.   1 2 3 4 5 6 7
15. I am great at turning problems into opportunities.   1 2 3 4 5 6 7
16. I can spot a good opportunity long before others can.   1 2 3 4 5 6 7
17. If I see someone in trouble, I help out in any way I can.   1 2 3 4 5 6 7

Source: T.S. Bateman and J.M. Crant, "The Proactive Component of Organizational Behavior: A Measure and Correlates," *Journal of Organizational Behavior*, March 1993, pp. 103-18; and J.M. Crant, "The Proactive Personality Scale as a Predictor of Entrepreneurial Intentions," *Journal of Small Business Management*, July 1996, pp. 42-49.

Scoring Key

To calculate your proactive personality score, add up your responses to all statements except item 3. For item 3, reverse your score.

Analysis and Interpretation

This instrument assesses proactive personality. That is, it identifies differences among people in the extent to which they take action to influence their environment. Proactive personalities identify opportunities and act on them; they show initiative, take action, and persevere until they bring about change. Research finds that the proactive personality is positively associated with entrepreneurial intentions.

Your total score will range between 17 and 119. The higher your score, the stronger your proactive personality. For instance, scores above 85 indicate fairly high proactivity.

A number of factors have been found to be associated with becoming an entrepreneur. For instance, entrepreneurship tends to flourish in communities that encourage risk taking and minimize the penalties attached to failures. Having supportive parents is additionally a plus. Entrepreneurs typically have parents who encouraged them to achieve, be independent, and take responsibility for their actions. Entrepreneurs also tend to have parents who were self-employed or entrepreneurs themselves. But a high score on this questionnaire suggests you have strong inclinations toward becoming an entrepreneur.

II.A.1: What's My Face-to-Face Communication Style?

Instrument

Respond to the 45 statements using the following scale:

    +2 = Strongly agree
    +1 = Agree
     0 = Neither agree or disagree
    -1 = Disagree
    -2 = Strongly disagree

1. I am comfortable with all varieties of people.	+2	+1	0	-1	-2
2. I laugh easily.	+2	+1	0	-1	-2
3. I readily express admiration for others.	+2	+1	0	-1	-2
4. What I say usually leaves an impression on people.	+2	+1	0	-1	-2
5. I leave people with an impression of me which they definitely tend to remember.	+2	+1	0	-1	-2
6. To be friendly, I habitually acknowledge verbally other's contributions.	+2	+1	0	-1	-2
7. I have some nervous mannerisms in my speech.	+2	+1	0	-1	-2
8. I am a very relaxed communicator.	+2	+1	0	-1	-2
9. When I disagree with somebody, I am very quick to challenge them.	+2	+1	0	-1	-2
10. I can always repeat back to a person exactly what was meant.	+2	+1	0	-1	-2
11. The sound of my voice is very easy to recognize.	+2	+1	0	-1	-2
12. I leave a definite impression on people.	+2	+1	0	-1	-2
13. The rhythm or flow of my speech is sometimes affected by nervousness.	+2	+1	0	-1	-2
14. Under pressure I come across as a relaxed speaker.	+2	+1	0	-1	-2
15. My eyes reflect exactly what I am feeling when I communicate.	+2	+1	0	-1	-2
16. I dramatize a lot.	+2	+1	0	-1	-2
17. Usually, I deliberately react in such a way that people know that I am listening to them.	+2	+1	0	-1	-2
18. Usually, I do not tell people much about myself until I get to know them well.	+2	+1	0	-1	-2
19. Regularly, I tell jokes, anecdotes, and stories when I communicate.	+2	+1	0	-1	-2
20. I tend to constantly gesture when I communicate.	+2	+1	0	-1	-2
21. I am an extremely open communicator.	+2	+1	0	-1	-2
22. I am vocally a loud communicator.	+2	+1	0	-1	-2
23. In arguments I insist upon very precise definitions.	+2	+1	0	-1	-2
24. In most social situations I generally speak very frequently.	+2	+1	0	-1	-2
25. I like to be strictly accurate when I communicate.	+2	+1	0	-1	-2

26. Because I have a loud voice, I can easily break

into a conversation.	+2	+1	0	-1	-2
27. Often I physically and vocally act out when I want to communicate.	+2	+1	0	-1	-2
28. I have an assertive voice.	+2	+1	0	-1	-2
29. I readily reveal personal things about myself.	+2	+1	0	-1	-2
30. I am dominant in social situations.	+2	+1	0	-1	-2
31. I am very argumentative.	+2	+1	0	-1	-2
32. Once I get wound up in a heated discussion I have a hard time stopping myself.	+2	+1	0	-1	-2
33. I am always an extremely friendly communicator.	+2	+1	0	-1	-2
34. I really like to listen very carefully to people.	+2	+1	0	-1	-2
35. Very often I insist that other people document or present some kind of proof for what they are arguing.	+2	+1	0	-1	-2
36. I try to take charge of things when I am with people.	+2	+1	0	-1	-2
37. It bothers me to drop an argument that is not resolved.	+2	+1	0	-1	-2
38. In most social situations I tend to come on strong.	+2	+1	0	-1	-2
39. I am very expressive nonverbally in social situations.	+2	+1	0	-1	-2
40. The way I say something usually leaves an impression on people.	+2	+1	0	-1	-2
41. Whenever I communicate, I tend to be very encouraging to people.	+2	+1	0	-1	-2
42. I actively use a lot of facial expressions when I communicate.	+2	+1	0	-1	-2
43. I very frequently verbally exaggerate to emphasize a point.	+2	+1	0	-1	-2
44. I am an extremely attentive communicator.	+2	+1	0	-1	-2
45. As a rule, I openly express my feelings and emotions.	+2	+1	0	-1	-2

Source: Adapted from R.W. Norton, "Foundation of a Communicator Style Construct," *Human Communication Research*, Vol. 4, No. 2, 1978, pp. 99-111. Copyright c 1978 International Communication Assoc., Inc. With permission of Sage Publications, Inc.

Scoring Key

Listed below are the statements that apply to each of the nine dimensions. Add up your scores (+2, +1, etc) for each dimension and divide by the number of statements. For items marked with an asterisk (*), reverse the score.

> Dominant = Items 22, 24, 26, 30, 36, 38
> Dramatic = 16, 19, 27, 28, 43
> Contentious = 9, 23, 25, 31, 32, 35, 37
> Animated = 15, 20, 39, 42
> Impression leaving = 4, 5, 11, 12, 40
> Relaxed = 1, 7*, 8, 13*, 14
> Attentive = 3, 10, 17, 34, 44
> Open = 18* 21, 29, 45
> Friendly = 2, 6, 33, 41

Analysis and Interpretation

There are nine dimensions of communication style. They are described as follows, with minimum and maximum possible scores on this assessment:

Dominant. Tends to take charge of social interactions (Min. score = -12, Max. score = 12)

Dramatic. Manipulates and exaggerates stories and uses other stylistic devices to highlight content. (Min. score = -10, Max. score = 10)

Contentious: Argumentative. (Min. score = -14, Max. score = 14)

Animated: Frequent and sustained eye contact, uses many facial expressions, and gestures often. (Min. score = -8, Max. score = 8)

Impression leaving: Are you remembered because of the communicative stimuli that you projected? (Min. score = -10, Max. score = 10)

Relaxed: Are you relaxed and void of nervousness? (Min. score = -10, Max. score = 10. Answers to Items 7 and 13 are reverse-scored.)

Attentive: Makes sure that the other person knows that he or she is being listened to. (Min. score = -10, Max. score = 10)

Open: Being conversational, expansive, affable, convivial, gregarious, unreserved, somewhat frank, definitely extroverted, and obviously approachable. (Min. score = -8, Max. score = 8. Answer to Item 18 is reverse-scored.)

Friendly: From being non-hostile to deep intimacy. (Min. score = -8, Max. score =8)

The higher your score for any dimension, the more that dimension characterizes your communication style. When you review your results, consider to what degree your scores aid or hinder your communication effectiveness. High scores for being attentive and open would almost always be positive qualities. A high score for contentious, on the other hand, could be a negative in many situations. In addition, your scores might offer guidance in choosing a career. For instance, a high score on friendliness would likely be a good match for customer-service jobs, while a high score on contentiousness might be a valuable asset for a trial lawyer.

II.A.2: How Good Are My Listening Skills?

Instrument

Respond to each of the 15 statements using the following scale:

        1 = Strongly agree
        2 = Agree
        3 = Neither agree or disagree
        4 = Disagree
        5 = Strongly disagree

1. I frequently attempt to listen to several conversations at the same time.   1 2 3 4 5
2. I like people to give me only the facts and then let me make my own interpretation.   1 2 3 4 5
3. I sometimes pretend to pay attention to people.   1 2 3 4 5
4. I consider myself a good judge of nonverbal communications.   1 2 3 4 5
5. I usually know what another person is going to say before he or she says it.   1 2 3 4 5
6. I usually end conversations that don't interest me by diverting my attention from the speaker.   1 2 3 4 5
7. I frequently nod, frown, or provide other nonverbal cues to let the speaker know how I feel about what he or she is saying.   1 2 3 4 5
8. I usually respond immediately when someone has finished talking   1 2 3 4 5
9. I evaluate what is being said while it is being said.   1 2 3 4 5
10. I usually formulate a response while the other person is still talking.   1 2 3 4 5
11. The speaker's "delivery" style frequently keeps me from listening to content.   1 2 3 4 5
12. I usually ask people to clarify what they have said rather than guess at the meaning.   1 2 3 4 5
13. I make a concerted effort to understand other people's points of view.   1 2 3 4 5
14. I frequently hear what I expect to hear rather than what is said.   1 2 3 4 5
15. Most people feel that I have understood their point of view when we disagree.   1 2 3 4 5

Source: Adapted from E.C. Glenn and E.A. Pood, "Listening Self-Inventory," *Supervisory Management*, January 1989, pp. 12-15. Used with permission of publisher; c 1989 American Management Association, New York.

Scoring Key

You score this instrument by summing up your responses for all items; however, you need to reverse your scores (5 becomes 1, 4 becomes 2, etc.) for statements 4, 12, 13, and 15.

Analysis and Interpretation

Effective communicators have developed good listening skills. This instrument is designed to provide you with some insights into your listening skills.

Scores range from 15 to 75. The higher your score, the better listener you are. While any cutoffs are essentially arbitrary, if you score 60 or above, your listening skills are fairly well honed. Scores of 40 or less indicate you need to make a serious effort at improving your listening skills. Good sources to help you improve your listening skills include: M. Helgesen, *Active Listening: Building Skills for Understanding* (Cambridge University Press, 1994); M. Burley-Allen, *Listening: The Forgotten Skill* (Wiley, 1995); and J.E. Sullivan, *The Good Listener* (Ave Maria Press, 2000).

II.B.1: What's My Leadership Style?

Instrument
The following items describe aspects of leadership behavior. Respond to each item according to the way you would be most likely to act if you were the leader of a work group. Use this scale for your responses:

> N = Never
> S = Seldom
> O = Occasionally
> F = Frequently
> A = Always

	N	S	O	F	A
1. I would most likely act as the spokesperson of the group.	N	S	O	F	A
2. I would encourage overtime work.	N	S	O	F	A
3. I would allow members complete freedom in their work.	N	S	O	F	A
4. I would encourage the use of uniform procedures.	N	S	O	F	A
5. I would permit the members to use their own judgment in solving problems.	N	S	O	F	A
6. I would stress being ahead of competing groups.	N	S	O	F	A
7. I would speak as a representative of the group.	N	S	O	F	A
8. I would needle members for greater effort.	N	S	O	F	A
9. I would try out my ideas in the group.	N	S	O	F	A
10. I would let the members do their work the way they think best.	N	S	O	F	A
11. I would be working hard for a promotion.	N	S	O	F	A
12. I would be able to tolerate postponement and uncertainty.	N	S	O	F	A
13. I would speak for the group when visitors were present.	N	S	O	F	A
14. I would keep the work moving at a rapid pace.	N	S	O	F	A
15. I would turn the members loose on a job and let them go to it.	N	S	O	F	A
16. I would settle conflicts when they occur in the group.	N	S	O	F	A
17. I would get swamped by details.	N	S	O	F	A
18. I would represent the group at outside meetings.	N	S	O	F	A
19. I would be reluctant to allow the members any freedom of action.	N	S	O	F	A
20. I would decide what shall be done and how it shall be done.	N	S	O	F	A
21. I would push for increased production.	N	S	O	F	A

22. I would let some members have authority

that I should keep.	N	S	O	F	A
23. Things would usually turn out as I predict.	N	S	O	F	A
24. I would allow the group a high degree of initiative.	N	S	O	F	A
25. I would assign group members to particular tasks.	N	S	O	F	A
26. I would be willing to make changes.	N	S	O	F	A
27. I would ask the members to work harder.	N	S	O	F	A
28. I would trust the group members to exercise good judgment.	N	S	O	F	A
29. I would schedule the work to be done.	N	S	O	F	A
30. I would refuse to explain my actions.	N	S	O	F	A
31. I would persuade others that my ideas are to their advantage.	N	S	O	F	A
32. I would permit the group to set its own pace.	N	S	O	F	A
33. I would urge the group to beat its previous record.	N	S	O	F	A
34. I would act without consulting the group.	N	S	O	F	A
35. I would ask that group members follow standard rules and regulations.	N	S	O	F	A

Source: J.W. Pfeiffer and J.E. Jones, eds., *A Handbook of Structural Experiences for Human Relations Training*, Vol. 1 (Revised). San Diego, CA: University Associates Press, 1974. Used with permission.

Scoring Key
To calculate your task-people score:
1. Circle the item number for items 8, 12, 17, 18, 19, 20, 34, and 35.
2. Write the number 1 in front of a *circled item number* if you responded S or N to that item.
3. Also write a number 1 in front of *item numbers not circled* if you responded A or F.
4. Circle the number 1's that you have written in front of the following items: 3, 5, 8, 10, 15, 18, 19, 22, 24, 26, 28, 30, 32, 34, and 35.
5. *Count the circled number* 1's. This is your score for concern for people.
6. *Count the uncircled number* 1's. This is your score for concern for task.

Analysis and Interpretation
This leadership instrument taps the degree to which you're task or people-oriented. Task-orientation is concerned with getting the job done, while people-orientation focuses on group interactions and the needs of individual members.

The cutoff scores separating high and low scores are approximately as follows. For task-orientation: High is a score above 10; low is below 10. For people-orientation: High is a score above 7; low is below 7.

The best leaders are ones that can balance their task/people orientation to various situations. A high score on both would indicate this balance. If you're too task-oriented, you tend to be autocratic. You get the job done, but at a high emotional cost. If you're too people-oriented, your leadership style may be overly laissez-faire. People are likely to be happy in their work but sometimes at the expense of productivity.

Your score should also help you to put yourself in situations that increase your likelihood of success. So, for instance, evidence indicates that when employees are experienced and know their jobs well, they tend to perform best with a people-oriented leader. If you're people-oriented, then this is a favorable situation for you. But if you're task-oriented, you might want to pass on this situation.

II.B.2: How Charismatic Am I?

Instrument
The statements on your right refer to the possible ways in which you might behave toward others when you are in a leadership role. For each statement, choose the response that best applies to you. Use this scale for your responses:

> 1 = To little or no extent
> 2 = To a slight extent
> 3 = To a moderate extent
> 4 = To a considerable extent
> 5 = To a very great extent

	1	2	3	4	5
1. I would pay close attention to what others say when they are talking.	1	2	3	4	5
2. I communicate clearly.	1	2	3	4	5
3. I am trustworthy.	1	2	3	4	5
4. I care about other people.	1	2	3	4	5
5. I don't put excessive energy into avoiding failure.	1	2	3	4	5
6. I make the work of others more meaningful.	1	2	3	4	5
7. I seem to focus on the key issues in situations.	1	2	3	4	5
8. I get across my meaning effectively, often in unusual ways.	1	2	3	4	5
9. I can be relied on to follow through on commitments.	1	2	3	4	5
10. I have a great deal of self-respect.	1	2	3	4	5
11. I enjoy taking carefully calculated risks.	1	2	3	4	5
12. I help others feel more competent in what they do.	1	2	3	4	5
13. I have a clear set of priorities.	1	2	3	4	5
14. I am in touch with how others feel.	1	2	3	4	5
15. I rarely change once I have taken a clear position.	1	2	3	4	5
16. I focus on strengths, of myself and of others.	1	2	3	4	5
17. I seem most alive when deeply involved in some project.	1	2	3	4	5
18. I show others that they are all part of the same group.	1	2	3	4	5
19. I get others to focus on the issues I see as important.	1	2	3	4	5
20. I communicate feelings as well as ideas.	1	2	3	4	5
21. I let others know where I stand.	1	2	3	4	5
22. I seem to know just how I "fit" into a group.	1	2	3	4	5
23. I learn from mistakes, do not treat errors as disasters, but as learning.	1	2	3	4	5
24. I am fun to be around.	1	2	3	4	5

Source: Adapted from M. Sashkin and W.C. Morris, *Experiencing Management*, c 1987 by Addison-Wesley Publishing Co., Inc. With permission.

Analysis and Interpretation

Charismatic leaders are ones whom followers perceive as having heroic or extraordinary leadership abilities. They tend to have high self-confidence and strong convictions about their beliefs. And followers are attracted to charismatic-types.

The authors of this instrument propose that it taps six basic leadership patterns:

Management of attention. How close attention do you pay to people with whom you are communicating? Do they have clear ideas about the relative importance of priorities? **Add up score on items 1, 7, 13, 19.**

Management of meaning. How effective are you at getting your meaning across? **Add up score on items 2, 8, 14, 20.**

Management of trust. Are you perceived as willing to follow through on promises and take clear positions on issues? **Add up score on items 3, 9, 15, 21.**

Management of self. How concerned are you about the welfare of others, their feelings, and your own self-regard? **Add up score on items 4, 10, 16, 22.**

Management of risk. Are you willing to take risks for those things you believe in? Are you willing to accept some failures in pursuit of your goals? **Add up score on items 5, 11, 17, 23.**

Management of feelings. Can you tap into the feelings of others and make their work more meaningful for them? **Add up score on items 6, 12, 18, 24.**

Your score on each dimension will range from 4 to 20. The higher your score , the more you demonstrate charismatic leader behaviors. While no specific cut-offs were stated by the authors, it seems reasonable to conclude that total scores of 85 or higher would indicate fairly strong charismatic qualities.

Not everyone is, or needs to be, a charismatic leader. Use your score as a guide to whether others will see you as charismatic. Additionally, if you want to project a more charismatic image, focus on behaviors where your score could be improved. For specific guidance in developing charismatic behaviors, you should read J.M. Howell and P.J. Frost, "A Laboratory Study of Charismatic Leadership," *Organizational Behavior and Human Decision Processes*, April 1989, pp. 243-69.

II.B.3: Do I Trust Others?

Instrument

For each of the five statements, indicate which of the two responses fit you best.

1. Some people say that most people can be trusted. Others say you can't be too careful in your dealings with people. How do you feel about it?
   a. Most people can be trusted.
   b. You can't be too careful.
2. Would you say that most people are more inclined to help others, or more inclined to look out for themselves?
   a. To help others.
   b. To look out for themselves.
3. If you don't watch yourself, people will take advantage of you.
   a. Agree
   b. Disagree
4. No one is going to care much what happens to you, when you get right down to it.
   a. Agree
   b. Disagree
5. Human nature is fundamentally cooperative.
   a. Agree
   b. Disagree

Source: M. Rosenberg, Faith in People, in *Occupations and Values* (Glencoe, Illinois: Free Press, 1957). Copyright 1957 by The Free Press, Division of the Macmillan Co.

Scoring Key

Give one point for each of the following answers: (1) b; (2) b; (3) a; (4) a; (5) b. Students scores will range between 1 and 5.

Analysis and Interpretation

This instrument was designed to test your faith in people. Scores will range from 1 (high faith) to 5 (low faith).

Based on results from more than 4200 students, you can compare your score with theirs:

1 = 16%
2 = 29%
3 = 25%
4 = 18%
5 = 12%

The research with students also found that those with high faith-in-people (low scores) were more likely to choose college majors consistent with people-oriented occupations—social work, human resources, and teaching. Those with low faith-in-people (high scores) were more likely to choose majors such as sales-promotion, business finance, and advertising.

There is no "right" answer to this test. Either extreme has its negatives. Those with low scores may be naive and susceptible to being taken advantage of. Those with high scores are likely to have trouble trusting others, working on teams, or acting as an empowering leader.

II.B.4: Do Others See Me as Trustworthy?

Instrument

For each of the nine statements, respond using one of these answers:

      1 = Strongly disagree
      2 = Disagree
      3 = Slightly disagree
      4 = Neither agree nor disagree
      5 = Slightly agree
      6 = Agree
      7 = Strongly agree

I am seen as someone who:

1. Is reliable.		1 2 3 4 5 6 7
2. Is always honest.		1 2 3 4 5 6 7
3. Succeeds by stepping on other people.		1 2 3 4 5 6 7
4. Tries to get the upper hand.		1 2 3 4 5 6 7
5. Takes advantage of others' problems.		1 2 3 4 5 6 7
6. Keeps my word.		1 2 3 4 5 6 7
7. Doesn't mislead others.		1 2 3 4 5 6 7
8. Tries to get out of my commitments.		1 2 3 4 5 6 7
9. Takes advantage of people who are vulnerable.		1 2 3 4 5 6 7

Source: Based on P. Bromiley and L. Cummings, "The Organizational Trust Inventory," in R.M. Kramer and T.R. Tyler, *Trust in Organizations* (Thousand Oaks, CA: Sage, 1996), pp. 328-29.

Scoring Key

To calculate your trusting score, add up reponses to items 1, 2, 6, and 7. For the other five items, reverse the score (7 becomes 1, 6 becomes 2, etc.). Now add up total results.

Analysis and Interpretation

Effective leaders have built a trusting relationship between themselves and those they seek to lead. This instrument provides you with insights into how trustworthy others are likely to perceive you.

Your total trustworthy score will range between 9 and 63. The higher your score, the more you're perceived as a person who can be trusted. Scores of 45 or higher suggest others are likely to perceive you as trustworthy; while scores below 27 suggest that people will not see you as someone who can be trusted.

If you want to build trust with others, look at the behaviors this instrument taps. Then think about what you can do to improve your score on each. Examples might include: being more open, speaking your feelings, giving generous credit to others, telling the truth, showing fairness and consistency, following through on promises and commitments, and maintaining confidences.

II.B.5: How Good Am I at Disciplining Others?

Instrument
This test contains eight disciplining practices. For each statement, select the answer that best describes you. Remember to respond as you *have* behaved or *would* behave, not as you think you *should* behave. If you have no managerial experience, answer the statements assuming you are a manager. Use the following scale to express your response:

    1 = Usually
    2 = Sometimes
    3 = Seldom

When disciplining an employee:

1. I provide ample warning before taking formal action.	1	2	3
2. I wait for a pattern of infractions before calling it to the employee's attention.	1	2	3
3. Even after repeated offenses, I prefer informal discussion about correcting the problem rather than formal disciplinary action.	1	2	3
4. I delay confronting the employee about an infraction until his or her performance-appraisal review.	1	2	3
5. In discussing an infraction with the employee, my style and tone are serious.	1	2	3
6. I explicitly seek to allow the employee to explain his or her position.	1	2	3
7. I remain impartial in allocating punishment.	1	2	3
8. I allocate stronger penalties for repeated offenses.	1	2	3

Source: S. P. Robbins, *Training in InterPersonal Skills: TIPS for Managing People at Work* (Upper Saddle River, NJ: Prentice Hall, 1989), pp. 104-05.

Scoring Key
Add up the points for questions 2, 3, and 4. For the other 5 questions (1, 5, 6, 7 and 8), reverse score them by giving a "1" response 3 points and a "3" response 1 point.

Analysis and Interpretation
This instrument is based on the literature defining preferred discipline techniques. It is not a precise tool but it will give you some insights into how effective you might be in practicing discipline in the work place.

Your score on this test will range from 8 to 24. A score of 22 or higher indicates excellent skills at disciplining. You understand that effective discipline recognizes the need to provide ample warning, act in a timely fashion, use a calm and serious tone, be specific about the problem, keep the process impersonal, and that disciplinary action should be progressive and consider mitigating circumstances. Scores in the 19 to 21 range suggest some deficiencies. Scores below 19 indicate considerable room for improvement. If you scored below 19, you might want to learn how to do a better job at disciplining by, for example, reading J. A. Belohlav, *The Art of Disciplining Your Employees* (Englewood Cliffs, NJ: Prentice Hall, 1985).

II.B.6: How Good Am I at Building and Leading a Team?

Instrument

Use the following rating scale to respond to the 18 questions on building and leading an effective team:

      1 = Strongly disagree
      2 = Disagree
      3 = Slightly disagree
      4 = Slightly agree
      5 = Agree
      6 = Strongly agree

1. I am knowledgeable about the different stages of development that teams can go through in their life cycles.   1 2 3 4 5 6

2. When a team forms, I make certain that all team members are introduced to one another at the outset.   1 2 3 4 5 6

3. When the team first comes together, I provide directions, answer team members' questions, and clarify goals, expectations, and procedures.   1 2 3 4 5 6

4. I help team members establish a foundation of trust among one another and between themselves and me.   1 2 3 4 5 6

5. I ensure that standards of excellence--not mediocrity or mere acceptability--characterize the team's work.   1 2 3 4 5 6

6. I provide a great deal of feedback to team members regarding their performance.   1 2 3 4 5 6

7. I encourage team members to balance individual autonomy with interdependence among other team members.   1 2 3 4 5 6

8. I help team members become at least as committed to the success of the team as to their own personal success.   1 2 3 4 5 6

9. I help members learn to play roles that assist the team in accomplishing its tasks as well as building strong interpersonal relationships.   1 2 3 4 5 6

10. I articulate a clear, exciting, passionate vision of what the team can achieve.   1 2 3 4 5 6

11. I help team members become committed to the team vision.   1 2 3 4 5 6

12. I encourage a win/win philosophy in the team; that is, when one member wins, every member wins.   1 2 3 4 5 6

13. I help the team avoid "groupthink" or making the group's survival more important than accomplishing its goal.   1 2 3 4 5 6

14. I use formal process management procedures to help the group become faster, more efficient, and more productive, and to prevent errors.   1 2 3 4 5 6

15. I encourage team members to represent the team's vision, goals, and accomplishments to outsiders.   1 2 3 4 5 6

16. I diagnose and capitalize on the team's core competence.   1 2 3 4 5 6

17. I encourage the team to achieve dramatic breakthrough

innovations as well as small continuous improvements.   1   2   3   4   5   6

18. I help the team work toward preventing mistakes, not just
correcting them after-the-fact.   1   2   3   4   5   6

Source: Adapted from D.A. Whetten and K.S. Cameron, *Developing Management Skills*, 3rd ed. (New York: HarperCollins, 1995), pp. 534-35.

Scoring Key

To calculate your total score, add up your scores on the 18 individual items.

Analysis and Interpretation

The authors of this instrument propose that it assesses team development behaviors in five areas: diagnosing team development (items 1, 16); managing the forming stage (2-4); managing the conforming stage (6-9, 13); managing the storming stage (10-12, 14, 15), and managing the performing stage (5, 17, 18). Your score will range between 18 and 108.

Based on a norm group of 500 business students, the following can help estimate where you are relative to others:

Total score of 95 or above	=	You're in the top quartile
72-94	=	You're in the second quartile
60-71	=	You're in the third quartile
Below 60	=	You're in the bottom quartile

If you need to work on your team-building skills, see S.A. Mohrman, S.G. Cohen, and A.M. Mohrman, Jr., *Designing Team-Based Organizations* (Jossey-Bass, 1995).

II.C.1: How Power-Oriented Am I?

Instrument
For each of statement, select the response that most closely resembles your attitude.
Use the following ratings scale for your responses:

1 = Disagree a lot
2 = Disagree a little
3 = Neutral
4 = Agree a little
5 = Agree a lot

1. The best way to handle people is to tell them what they want to hear.	1	2	3	4	5
2. When you ask someone to do something for you, it is best to give the real reason for wanting it rather than giving reasons that might carry more weight.	1	2	3	4	5
3. Anyone who completely trusts anyone else is asking for trouble.	1	2	3	4	5
4. It is hard to get ahead without cutting corners here and there.	1	2	3	4	5
5. It is safest to assume that all people have a vicious streak, and it will come out when they are given a chance.	1	2	3	4	5
6. One should take action only when it is morally right.	1	2	3	4	5
7. Most people are basically good and kind.	1	2	3	4	5
8. There is no excuse for lying to someone else.	1	2	3	4	5
9. Most people more easily forget the death of their father than the loss of their property.	1	2	3	4	5
10. Generally speaking, people won't work hard unless they're forced to do so.	1	2	3	4	5

Source: R. Christie and F.L. Geis, *Studies in Machiavellianism*. c Academic Press 1970. With permission.

Scoring Key
To obtain your score, add your responses to questions 1, 3, 4, 5, 9, and 10. For the other four questions, reverse your scores (5 becomes 1, 4 becomes 2, and so on).

Analysis and Interpretation
This instrument was designed to compute your Machiavellianism (Mach) score. Machiavelli wrote in the 16th century on how to gain and manipulate power. An individual with a high-Mach score is pragmatic, maintains emotional distance, and believes that ends can justify means. The National Opinion Research Center, which used this instrument in a random sample of American adults, found that the national average was 25.

High-Machs are more likely to manipulate more, win more, are persuaded less, and persuade others more than do low-Machs. High-Machs are also more likely to shade the truth or act unethically in ambiguous situations where the outcome is important to them.

II.C.2: What's My Preferred Type of Power?

Instrument
Respond to the 20 statements by thinking in terms of how you prefer to influence others. Use the following scale for your answers:

        1 = Strongly disagree
        2 = Disagree
        3 = Neither agree or disagree
        4 = Agree
        5 = Strongly agree

To influence others, I would prefer to:

	1	2	3	4	5
1. Increase their pay level	1	2	3	4	5
2. Make them feel valued	1	2	3	4	5
3. Give undesirable job assignments	1	2	3	4	5
4. Make them feel like I approve of them	1	2	3	4	5
5. Make them feel that they have commitments to meet	1	2	3	4	5
6. Make them feel personally accepted	1	2	3	4	5
7. Make them feel important	1	2	3	4	5
8. Give them good technical suggestions	1	2	3	4	5
9. Make the work difficult for them	1	2	3	4	5
10. Share my experience and/or training	1	2	3	4	5
11. Make things unpleasant here	1	2	3	4	5
12. Make being at work distasteful	1	2	3	4	5
13. Influence their getting a pay increase	1	2	3	4	5
14. Make them feel like they should satisfy their job requirements	1	2	3	4	5
15. Provide them with sound job-related advice	1	2	3	4	5
16. Provide them with special benefits	1	2	3	4	5
17. Influence their getting a promotion	1	2	3	4	5
18. Give them the feeling that they have responsibilities to fulfill	1	2	3	4	5
19. Provide them with needed technical knowledge	1	2	3	4	5
20. Make them recognize that they have tasks to accomplish	1	2	3	4	5

Source: Adapted from T.R. Hinken and C.A. Schriesheim, "Development and Application of New Scales to Measure the French and Raven (1959) Bases of Social Power," *Journal of Applied Psychology*, August 1989, pp. 561-67.

Scoring Key

To get your score for each base, calculate as follows:

> Reward = Add up your responses to items 1, 13, 16, 17; then divide by 4.
> Coercive = Add up your responses to items 3, 9, 11, 12; then divide by 4.
> Legitimate = Add up your responses to items 5, 14, 18, and 20; then divide by 4.
> Expert = Add up your responses to items 8, 10, 15, and 19; then divide by 4.
> Referent = Add up your responses to items 2, 4, 6, and 7; then divide by 4.

Analysis and Interpretation

Five bases of power have been identified: reward (based on the ability to distribute valuable rewards); coercive (based on fear); legitimate (based on formal position); expert (based on possessing knowledge or skill); and referent (based on others' desire to identify with you).

A high score (4 or greater) on any of the five dimensions implies that you prefer to influence others by using that particular form of power. A low score (2 or less) suggests that you prefer not to employ this power base.

Managerial positions come with legitimate, reward, and coercive powers. However, you don't have to be a manager to have power. If you're not in a position of formal authority, you can still be a powerful person in your organization if you focus on developing your expert and referent power bases.

II.C.3: How Good Am I at Playing Politics?

<u>**Instrument**</u>
Using the following 7-point scale, indicate the response that best describes how much you agree or disagree with each of the 18 statements.

> 1 = Strongly disagree
> 2 = Disagree
> 3 = Slightly disagree
> 4 = Neutral
> 5 = Slightly agree
> 6 = Agree
> 7 = Strongly agree

1. I spend a lot of time and effort making connections, working relationships, and networking with others.   1   2   3   4   5   6   7
2. I am able to make most people feel comfortable and at ease around me.   1   2   3   4   5   6   7
3. I am able to communicate easily and effectively with others. 1   2   3   4   5   6   7
4. It is easy for me to develop good rapport with most people. 1   2   3   4   5   6   7
5. I understand people very well.   1   2   3   4   5   6   7
6. I am good at building relationships with influential people at work.   1   2   3   4   5   6   7
7. I am particularly good at sensing the motivations and hidden agendas of others.   1   2   3   4   5   6   7
8. When communicating with others, it is important that they believe I am genuine and sincere in what I say and do.   1   2   3   4   5   6   7
9. I have developed a large network of colleagues and associates at work who I can call on for support when I really need to get things done.   1   2   3   4   5   6   7
10. I know a lot of important people and am well connected at work.   1   2   3   4   5   6   7
11. I spend a lot of time at work developing connections and networking with others.   1   2   3   4   5   6   7
12. I am good at getting people to like me.   1   2   3   4   5   6   7
13. It is important that I make people believe I am genuine and sincere in what I say and do.   1   2   3   4   5   6   7
14. I try to show a genuine interest in other people.   1   2   3   4   5   6   7
15. I am good at using my connections and network to make things happen at work.   1   2   3   4   5   6   7
16. I have good intuition or "savvy" about how to present myself to others.   1   2   3   4   5   6   7
17. I always seem to instinctively know the right things to say or do to influence others.   1   2   3   4   5   6   7
18. I pay close attention to peoples' facial expressions.   1   2   3   4   5   6   7

Source: G. R. Ferris, R. W. Kolodinsky, W. A. Hockwarter, and D. D. Frink, "Conceptualization, Measurement, and Validation of the Political Skill Construct," paper presented at the 61st National Academy of Management Conference; Washington, D.C., August 2001. With permission.

Scoring Key

To calculate your score, add up the scores for the 18 items.

Analysis and Interpretation

The authors of this instrument define political skill as "an interpersonal style construct that combines social perceptiveness or astuteness with the capacity to adjust one's behavior to different and changing situational demands in a manner that inspires trust, confidence, and genuineness, and effectively influences and controls the responses of others." They have broken this down into four dimensions: *Self and social astuteness* is the ability to astutely observe others and to be keenly attuned to diverse social situations. *Interpersonal influence/control* is the ability to exert a powerful influence on others. *Network building/social capital* is being adept at developing and using diverse networks of people. And *genuineness/sincerity* is the ability to appear to others as having high integrity, authenticity, and sincerity. The 18-items in this instrument tap these four dimensions.

Your score will range between 18 and 126. The higher your score, the better your political skills. That is, the better you are at not only knowing precisely what to do in different social situations at work but exactly how to do it in a sincere, engaging manner that disguises any ulterior, self-serving motives. The authors don't provide any specific cut-off scores but we suggest that scores below 72 indicate that you are a bit politically naïve and may have difficulty furthering your self-interests in an organization. Scores above 100 suggest you are quite effective in gaining the support and trust of others and using that to advance your agenda.

II.C.4: How Well Do I Manage Impressions?

Instrument

For each of the 22 strategies, describe how frequently you have used each in the last six months while at work. Use the following rating scale to record your answers:

        1 = Never behave this way
        2 = Seldom behave this way
        3 = Occasionally behave this way
        4 = Frequently behave this way
        5 = Often behave this way

1. Talk proudly about your experience or education.   1 2 3 4 5
2. Make people aware of your talents or qualifications.   1 2 3 4 5
3. Let others know that you're valuable to the organization.   1 2 3 4 5
4. Make people aware of your accomplishments.   1 2 3 4 5
5. Compliment your colleagues so they'll see you as likable.   1 2 3 4 5
6. Take an interest in your colleagues' personal lives to show them that you are friendly.   1 2 3 4 5
7. Praise your colleagues for their accomplishments so they'll consider you a nice person.   1 2 3 4 5
8. Do personal favors for your colleagues to show them that you're friendly.   1 2 3 4 5
9. Stay at work late so people will know you are hard working.   1 2 3 4 5
10. Try to appear busy, even at times when things are slower.   1 2 3 4 5
11. Arrive at work early in order to look dedicated.   1 2 3 4 5
12. Come to the office at night or on weekends to show that you're dedicated.   1 2 3 4 5
13. Be intimidating with coworkers when it will help you get your job done.   1 2 3 4 5
14. Let others know that you can make things difficult for them if they push you too far.   1 2 3 4 5
15. Deal forcefully with colleagues when they hamper your ability to get your job done.   1 2 3 4 5
16. Deal strongly or aggressively with coworkers who interfere in your business.   1 2 3 4 5
17. Use intimidation to get colleagues to behave appropriately.   1 2 3 4 5
18. Act like you know less than you do so people will help you out.   1 2 3 4 5
19. Try to gain assistance or sympathy from people by appearing needy in some area.   1 2 3 4 5
20. Pretend not to understand something to gain someone's help.   1 2 3 4 5
21. Act like you need assistance so people will help you out.   1 2 3 4 5
22. Pretend to know less than you do so you can avoid an unpleasant assignment.   1 2 3 4 5

Source; M.C. Bolino and W.H. Turnley, "Measuring Impression Management in Organizations: A Scale Development Based on the Jones and Pittman Taxonomy," working paper.

Scoring Key

To determine the degree to which you use the five impression management strategies, make the following calculations:

> Add up your scores for items 1-4 and divide by 4. This is your self-promotion score.
> Add up your scores for items 5-8 and divide by 4. This is your ingratiation score.
> Add up your scores for items 9-12 and divide by 4. This is your exemplification score.
> Add up your scores for items 13-17 and divide by 5. This is your intimidation score.
> Add up your scores for items 18-22 and divide by 5. This is your supplication score.

Analysis and Interpretation

Most of us are concerned with the image others have of us. Impression management is the process by which people attempt to control the impression others form of them.

This instrument assesses the degree to which you use five impression management strategies. Items 1 through 4 tap *self-promotion*—the extent to which you point out your abilities or accomplishments in order to be seen as competent by others. Items 5 through 8 assess *ingratiation*—the extent to which you do favors or use flattery in order to be seen as likable by others. Items 9 through 12 tap *exemplification*—the extent to which you engage in self-sacrifice or go above and beyond the call of duty in order to be viewed as dedicated by others. Items 13 through 17 assess *intimidation*—the extent to which you signal your power or potential to punish in order to be seen as dangerous by others. Finally, items 18 through 22 tap *supplication*—the extent to which you advertise your weaknesses or shortcomings in order to be viewed as needy by others.

The strategies with the highest scores are the ones you most often use. Consistent scores of 2.3 or less suggest you make little use of impression management techniques. In contrast, multiple scores of 3.5 or higher indicate active use of impression management. For comparative purposes, a survey of 147 professionals and managers who work for a Fortune 500 technology firm resulted in the following mean scores: self-promotion = 2.95; ingratiation = 2.95; exemplification = 2.29; intimidation = 1.91; and supplication = 1.62.

II.C.5: What's My Preferred Conflict-Handling Style?

Instrument

When you differ with someone, how do you respond? Use the following rating scale to record your answers:

   1 = Practically never
   2 = Once in a great while
   3 = Sometimes
   4 = Fairly often
   5 = Very often

1. I work to come out victorious, no matter what.	1	2	3	4	5
2. I try to put the needs of others above my own.	1	2	3	4	5
3. I look for a mutually satisfactory solution.	1	2	3	4	5
4. I try not to get involved in conflicts.	1	2	3	4	5
5. I strive to investigate issues thoroughly and jointly.	1	2	3	4	5
6. I never back away from a good argument.	1	2	3	4	5
7. I strive to foster harmony.	1	2	3	4	5
8. I negotiate to get a portion of what I propose.	1	2	3	4	5
9. I avoid open discussions of controversial subjects.	1	2	3	4	5
10. I openly share information with others in resolving disagreements.	1	2	3	4	5
11. I would rather win than end up compromising.	1	2	3	4	5
12. I got along with suggestions of others.	1	2	3	4	5
13. I look for a middle ground to resolve disagreements.	1	2	3	4	5
14. I keep my true opinions to myself to avoid hard feelings.	1	2	3	4	5
15. I encourage the open sharing of concerns and issues.	1	2	3	4	5
16. I am reluctant to admit I am wrong.	1	2	3	4	5
17. I try to help others avoid losing face in a disagreement.	1	2	3	4	5
18. I stress the advantages of give-and-take.	1	2	3	4	5
19. I agree early on, rather than argue about a point.	1	2	3	4	5
20. I state my position as only one point of view.	1	2	3	4	5

Source: Based on conflict dimensions defined in K.W. Thomas, "Conflict and Conflict Management," in M. Dunnette (ed.), *Handbook of Industrial and Organizational Psychology* (Chicago: Rand McNally, 1976), pp. 889-935.

To calculate your conflict-handling score, add up your totals for each of the five categories. Categories and corresponding items are listed below.

Analysis and Interpretation
Research has identified five conflict-handling styles. They are defined as follows:

Competing = A desire to satisfy one's interests, regardless of the impact on the other party to the conflict. Items 1, 6, 11, and 16 in this instrument tap this style.

Collaborating = Where the parties to a conflict each desire to satisfy fully the concerns of all parties. Items 5, 10, 15, and 20 in this instrument.

Avoiding = The desire to withdraw from or suppress the conflict. Items 4, 9, 14, and 19 in this instrument.

Accommodating = Willingness of one party in a conflict to place the opponent's Interests above his or her own. Items 2, 7, 12, and 17 in this instrument.

Compromising = Where each party to a conflict is willing to give up something. Items 3, 8, 13, and 18 in this instrument.

Your score within each category will range from 4 to 20. The category you score highest in is your preferred conflict-handling style. Your next-highest total is your secondary style.

Ideally, we should adjust our conflict-handling style to the situation. For instance, avoidance works well when a conflict is trivial, when emotions are running high and time is needed to cool them down, or when the potential disruption from a more assertive action outweighs the benefits of a resolution. In contrast, competing works well when you need a quick resolution on important issues where unpopular actions must be taken, or when commitment by others to your solution is not critical. But the evidence indicates that we all have a preferred style for handling conflicts. When "push comes to shove," this is the style we tend to rely on. Your score on this instrument provides you with insight into this preferred style. Use this information to work against your natural tendencies when the situation requires a different style.

To better match your conflict-handling style to the situation, see S.P. Robbins, *Managing Organizational Conflict: A Nontraditional Approach* (Prentice Hall, 1974).

II.C.6: What's My Negotiating Style?

Instrument
Listed below are seven characteristics related to a person's negotiating style. Each characteristic demonstrates a range of variation. Indicate your own preference by selecting a point along the 1-to-5 continuum for each characteristic.

1. Approach	Confrontational	1	2	3	4	5	Collaborative
2. Personality	Emotional	1	2	3	4	5	Rational
3. Formality	High	1	2	3	4	5	Low
4. Communication	Indirect	1	2	3	4	5	Direct
5. Candidness	Closed	1	2	3	4	5	Open
6. Search for options	Limited	1	2	3	4	5	Many
7. Willingness to use power	Low	1	2	3	4	5	High

Source: Based on R. Fisher and W. Ury, *Getting to Yes* (New York: Penguin, 1981); and J. W. Salacuse, "Ten Ways That Culture Affects Negotiating Style: Some Survey Results," *Negotiation Journal*, July 1998, pp. 221-39.

Scoring Key
To calculate your score, add up the scores for the 7 items

Analysis and Interpretation
People differ in the way they handle negotiations. This instrument attempts to tap the key dimensions that differentiate preferences in negotiation style.

Your score on this test will range between 7 and 35. Research indicates that negotiation style is influenced by a number of factors—including the situation, your cultural background, and your work occupation. Nevertheless, experts in negotiation generally recommend individuals use a style that will result in a high score on this test. That is, they favor collaboration, rationality, a direct communication style, etc. We think it best to consider your total score in a situational context. For instance, while a high total score may generally be favorable, the use of an informal style may be a handicap for North Americans or Europeans when negotiating with Nigerians, who favor high formality. Similarly, Latin Americans tend to show their emotions in negotiation. So if you're negotiating with Brazilians or Costa Ricans, a more emotional approach on your part may be appropriate or even expected.

III.A.1: What Type of Organization Structure Do I Prefer?

Instrument

Respond to each of the 15 statements by using one of the following numbers:

      1 = Strongly disagree
      2 = Disagree somewhat
      3 = Undecided
      4 = Agree somewhat
      5 = Strongly agree

I prefer to work in an organization where:

1. Goals are defined by those at higher levels.	1	2	3	4	5
2. Clear job descriptions exist for every job.	1	2	3	4	5
3. Top management makes important decisions.	1	2	3	4	5
4. Promotions and pay increases are based as much on length of service as on level of performance.	1	2	3	4	5
5. Clear lines of authority and responsibility are established.	1	2	3	4	5
6. My career is pretty well planned out for me.	1	2	3	4	5
7. I have a great deal of job security.	1	2	3	4	5
8. I can specialize.	1	2	3	4	5
9. My boss is readily available.	1	2	3	4	5
10. Organization rules and regulations are clearly specified.	1	2	3	4	5
11. Information rigidly follows the chain of command.	1	2	3	4	5
12. There is a minimal number of new tasks for me to learn.	1	2	3	4	5
13. Work groups incur little turnover in members.	1	2	3	4	5
14. People accept authority of a leader's position.	1	2	3	4	5
15. I am part of a group whose training and skills are similar to mine.	1	2	3	4	5

Source: Based on J.F. Veiga and J.N. Yanouzas, *The Dynamics of Organization Theory: Gaining a Macro Perspective* (St. Paul, MN: West, 1979), pp. 158-60.

Scoring Key

To calculate your score, add up your responses to all 15 items.

Analysis and Interpretation

This instrument measures your preference for working in a mechanistic or organic organization structure. Mechanistic structures are characterized by extensive departmentalization, high formalization, a limited information network, and centralization. In contrast, organic structures are flat, use cross-hierarchical and cross-functional teams, have low formalization, possess a comprehensive information network, and rely on participative decision making.

Scores above 60 suggest that you prefer a mechanistic design. Scores below 45 indicate a preference for an organic design. Scores between 45 and 60 suggest no clear preference.

Since the trend in recent years has been toward more organic designs, you're more likely to find a good organizational match if you score low on this instrument. But there are few, if any, pure organic structures. So very low scores may also mean that you're likely to be frustrated by what you perceive as overly rigid structures of rules, regulations, and boss-centered leadership. In general, however, low scores indicate that you prefer small, innovative, flexible, team-oriented organizations. And high scores indicate a preference for stable, rule-oriented, more bureaucratic organizations.

III.A.2: How Willing Am I to Delegate?

Instrument

Indicate the degree to which you agree or disagree with these 18 statements. If you have limited work experience, base your answers on what you know about yourself and your personal beliefs. Use the following scale for your responses:

        1 = Strongly disagree
        2 = Disagree
        3 = Neither agree or disagree
        4 = Agree
        5 = Strongly agree

1. I'd delegate more, but the jobs I delegate never seem to get done the way I want them to be done.   1   2   3   4   5

2. I don't feel I have the time to delegate properly.   1   2   3   4   5

3. I carefully check on subordinates' work without letting them know I'm doing it, so I can correct their mistakes if necessary before they cause too many problems.   1   2   3   4   5

4. I delegate the whole job--giving the opportunity for the subordinate to complete it without any of my involvement. Then I review the result.   1   2   3   4   5

5. When I have given clear instructions and the task isn't done right, I get upset.   1   2   3   4   5

6. I feel my staff lacks the commitment that I have. So any task I delegate won't get done as well as I'd do it.   1   2   3   4   5

7. I'd delegate more, but I feel I can do the task better than the person I might delegate it to.   1   2   3   4   5

8. I'd delegate more, but if the individual I delegate the task to does an incompetent job, I'll be seriously criticized.   1   2   3   4   5

9. If I were to delegate a task, my job wouldn't be nearly as much fun.   1   2   3   4   5

10. When I delegate a task, I often find that the outcome is such that I end up doing the task over again myself.   1   2   3   4   5

11. I have not really found that delegation saves any time.   1   2   3   4   5

12. I delegate a task clearly and concisely, explaining exactly how it should be accomplished.   1   2   3   4   5

13. I can't delegate as much as I'd like to because my subordinates lack the necessary experience.   1   2   3   4   5

14. I feel that when I delegate I lose control.   1   2   3   4   5

15. I would delegate more but I'm pretty much a perfectionist.	1	2	3	4	5
16. I work longer hours than I should.	1	2	3	4	5
17. I can give subordinates the routine tasks, but I feel I must keep nonroutine tasks to myself.	1	2	3	4	5
18. My own boss expects me to keep very close to all details of my job.	1	2	3	4	5

Source: Adapted from T.J. Klein, "How to Improve Delegation Habits," *Management Review*, May 1982, p. 59. With permission. c 1982 American Management Association.

Scoring Key
To calculate your score, total up your responses to the 18 items.

Analysis and Interpretation
Managers get things done through other people. To do so, they need to be able to delegate. But many managers have difficulty in delegating authority. This instrument taps most of the excuses new managers give for failing to delegate. It also addresses some of the errors used when delegation is done improperly.

Your scores can be interpreted as follows:

72 -90 points = Ineffective delegation
54-71 points = Delegation skills need substantial improvement
36-53 points = You still have room to improve
18-35 points = Superior delegation

To improve your delegation skills, see D.D. McConskey, *No-Nonsense Delegation* (AMACOM, 1974); and L.L. Steinmetz, *The Art and Skill of Delegation* (Addison-Wesley, 1976).

III.A.3: How Good Am I at Giving Performance Feedback?

Instrument

For each of the following pairs, identify the statement that most closely matches what you *normally* do when you give feedback to someone else on their job performance.

1. a. Describe the behavior
   b. Evaluate the behavior

2. a. Focus on the feelings that the behavior evokes
   b. Tell the person what they should be doing differently

3. a. Give specific instances of the behavior
   b. Generalize

4. a. Deal only with behavior that the person can control
   b. Sometimes focus on something the person can do nothing about

5. a. Tell the person as soon as possible after the behavior
   b. Sometimes wait too long

6. a. Focus on the effect the behavior has on me
   b. Try to figure out why the individual did what he or she did

7. a. Balance negative feedback with positive feedback
   b. Sometimes focus only on the negative

8. a. Do some soul searching to make sure that the reason I am giving the feedback is to help the other person or to strengthen our relationship
   b. Sometimes give feedback to punish, win against, or dominate the other person

Source: Adapted from L.A. Mainiero and C.L. Tromley, *Developing Managerial Skills in Organizational Behavior*, 2nd ed. (Englewood Cliffs, NJ: Prentice Hall, 1994), pp. 125-26. With permission.

Scoring Key

To calculate your score, add up how many "a" responses you totaled. Do the same for "b" responses.

Analysis and Interpretation

This instrument is designed to assess how good you are at providing performance feedback.

The "a" responses are your self-perceived strengths and the "b" responses are your self-perceived weaknesses. By looking at the proportion of your "a" and "b" responses, you will be able to see how effective you feel you are when giving performance feedback and determine where your strengths and weaknesses lie. For instance, an a/b ratio of 8/0, 7/1, or 6/2 suggests relatively strong feedback skills. In contrast, ratios of 3/5, 2/6, 1/7, or 0/8 indicate significant self-perceived weaknesses that can be improved upon. To work on improving your feedback skills, see M. London, *Job Feedback: Giving, Seeking, and Using Feedback for Performance Improvement* (Erlbaum, 1997).

III.B.1: What's the Right Organizational Culture For Me?

Instrument
For each of the seven statements, indicate your level of agreement or disagreement using the following scale:

         1 = Strongly disagree
         2 = Disagree
         3 = Uncertain
         4 = Agree
         5 = Strongly agree

1. I like the thrill and excitement from taking risks.	1	2	3	4	5
2. I prefer managers who provide detailed and rational explanations for their decisions.	1	2	3	4	5
3. If a person's job performance is inadequate, it's irrelevant how much effort he or she made.	1	2	3	4	5
4. No person's needs should be compromised in order for a department to achieve its goals.	1	2	3	4	5
5. I like being part of a team and having my performance assessed in terms of my contribution to the team.	1	2	3	4	5
6. I like to work where there isn't a great deal of pressure and where people are essentially easygoing.	1	2	3	4	5
7. I like things to be stable and predictable.	1	2	3	4	5

_____

Source: S.P. Robbins, *Organizational Behavior*, 8th ed. (Upper Saddle River, NJ: Prentice Hall, 1998), p. 617.

Scoring Key
To calculate your score, add up your responses. However, reverse your scores for items 2 and 7.

Analysis and Interpretation
This instrument taps the seven primary dimensions of an organization's culture: Innovation and risk taking; attention to detail; outcome orientation; people orientation; team orientation; aggressiveness; and stability.

Your total score will range between 7 and 35. Scores of 21 or lower indicate that you're more comfortable in a formal, mechanistic, rule-oriented, and structured culture. This is often associated with large corporations and government agencies. The lower your number, the stronger your preference for this type of culture. Scores above 22 indicate a preference for informal, humanistic, flexible, and innovative cultures, which are more likely to be found in high-tech companies, small businesses, research units, or advertising agencies. The higher your score above 22, the stronger your preference for these humanistic cultures.

Organizational cultures differ. So do individuals. The better you're able to match your personal preferences to an organization's culture, the more likely you are to find satisfaction in your work, the less likely you are to leave, and the greater the probability that you'll receive positive performance evaluations.

III.B.2: How Committed Am I to My Organization?

Instrument

Listed to the right are a series of statements that represent possible feelings that individuals might have about the organization for which they work. With respect to your own feelings about your employing organization, indicate the degree of your agreement or disagreement by using the following rating scale:

1 = Strongly disagree
2 = Moderately disagree
3 = Slightly disagree
4 = Neither agree or disagree
5 = Slightly agree
6 = Moderately agree
7 = Strongly agree

1. I am willing to put in a great deal of effort beyond that normally expected in order to help this organization be successful.　1 2 3 4 5 6 7

2. I talk up this organization to my friends as a great organization to work for.　1 2 3 4 5 6 7

3. I feel very little loyalty to this organization.　1 2 3 4 5 6 7

4. I would accept almost any type of job assignment in order to keep working for this organization.　1 2 3 4 5 6 7

5. I find that my values and the organization's values are very similar.　1 2 3 4 5 6 7

6. I am proud to tell others that I am part of this organization.　1 2 3 4 5 6 7

7. I could just as well be working for a different organization as long as the type of work was similar.　1 2 3 4 5 6 7

8. This organization really inspires the very best in me in the way of job performance.　1 2 3 4 5 6 7

9. It would take very little change in my present circumstances to cause me to leave this organization.　1 2 3 4 5 6 7

10. I am extremely glad that I chose this organization to work for over others I was considering at the time I joined.　1 2 3 4 5 6 7

11. There's not too much to be gained by sticking with this organization indefinitely.　1 2 3 4 5 6 7

12. Often, I find it difficult to agree with this organization's policies on important matters relating to its employees.　1 2 3 4 5 6 7

13. I really care about the fate of this organization.　1 2 3 4 5 6 7

14. For me this is the best of all possible organizations for which to work.　1 2 3 4 5 6 7

15. Deciding to work for this organization was a definite mistake on my part.　1 2 3 4 5 6 7

Source: R. Mowday and R.M. Steers, "The Measurement of Organizational Commitment," *Journal of Vocational Behavior*, April 1979, pp. 224-47.

Scoring Key

To calculate your total, add up your scores for the 15 items; however, reverse your scoring for items 3, 7, 9, 11, 12, and 15. Now divide the total by 15.

Analysis and Interpretation

This instrument taps your level of organizational commitment. That is, it assesses the relative strength of your identification with and involvement in your organization. High organizational commitment is characterized by a strong belief in and acceptance of your organization's goals and values; a willingness to exert considerable effort on behalf of your organization; and a strong desire to maintain membership in the organization.

Scores on this assessment range from 1-7. Studies using this instrument have found mean results in the 4.0 to 6.1 range. What does high or low organizational commitment indicate? Studies show that committed employees are less likely to leave their organization and are more likely to have lower absenteeism rates. Of course, given the changing relationship between employees and employers in the past 15 years, it would not be surprising to see your score lower than the mean range cited. It's probably fair to say that today's employees, as a group, are less committed to their employing organizations than their predecessors of a generation ago. In fact, a high score today may suggest rigidity on your part and inadequate planning of career options should your organization downsize as a result of financial setbacks, efficiency moves, or merger with another firm.

III.B.3: Am I Experiencing Work/Family Conflict?

Instrument
Identify the degree to which you agree or disagree with the eight statements by using the following rating scale:

> 1 = Strongly disagree
> 2 = Inclined to disagree
> 3 = Neither agree or disagree
> 4 = Inclined to agree
> 5 = Strongly agree

1. My work schedule often conflicts with my family life.	1	2	3	4	5
2. After work, I come home too tired to do some of the things I'd like to do.	1	2	3	4	5
3. On the job I have so much work to do that it takes away from my personal interests.	1	2	3	4	5
4. My family dislikes how often I am preoccupied with my work while I am home.	1	2	3	4	5
5. Because my work is demanding, at times I am irritable at home.	1	2	3	4	5
6. The demands of my job make it difficult to be relaxed all the time at home.	1	2	3	4	5
7. My work takes up time that I'd like to spend with my family.	1	2	3	4	5
8. My job makes it difficult to be the kind of spouse or parent I'd like to be.	1	2	3	4	5

Source: R.E. Kopelman, J.H. Greenhaus, and T.F. Connolly, "A Model of Work, Family, and Interrole Conflict: A Construct Validation Study," *Organizational Behavior and Human Performance*, October 1983, pp. 198-215.

Scoring Key
To calculate your work-family-conflict score, add up your responses to the eight items. All are stated negatively, so agreement is indicative of conflict.

Analysis and Interpretation
This instrument taps interrole conflict--the pressures of dealing with the interdependencies between work and family lives. Research has found that the most prevalent forms of work/family conflict are excessive work demands, schedule conflicts, and fatigue or irritability. These are addressed in this questionnaire.

Your score will range between 8 and 40; and the higher your score, the more conflict you seem to be experiencing.

In today's economy, where two-income families are the norm, both men and women increasingly complain about balancing the demands of work and family. So scores on this instrument are likely to be significantly higher today than a generation ago. Scores of 30 or above should be seen as a "red flag." You need to rethink your priorities since you seem to feel you are not fulfilling your responsibilities to your home and family.

III.B.4: How Motivated Am I to Manage?

Instrument
Complete this instrument by identifying your degree of agreement or disagreement. Use the following rating scale:

> 1 = Strongly disagree
> 2 = Moderately disagree
> 3 = Slightly disagree
> 4 = Neither agree or disagree
> 5 = Slightly agree
> 6 = Moderately agree
> 7 = Strongly agree

1. I have a generally positive attitude toward those holding positions of authority over me.　　1　2　3　4　5　6　7

2. I enjoy competition and striving to win for myself and my work group.　　1　2　3　4　5　6　7

3. I like to tell others what to do and have no problem with imposing sanctions to enforce my directives.　　1　2　3　4　5　6　7

4. I like being active, assertive, and protecting the members of my work group.　　1　2　3　4　5　6　7

5. I enjoy the idea of standing out from the group, behaving in a unique manner, and being highly visible.　　1　2　3　4　5　6　7

6. I am willing to perform routine, day-to-day administrative tasks and duties.　　1　2　3　4　5　6　7

Source: Based on J.B. Miner and N.R. Smith, "Decline and Stabilization of Managerial Motivation Over a 20-Year Period," *Journal of Applied Psychology*, June 1982, pp. 297-305; and J.B. Miner, B. Ebrahimi, and J.M. Wachtel, "How Deficiencies in Motivation to Manage Contribute to the United States' Competitiveness Problem (and What Can Be Done About It)," *Human Resource Management*, Fall 1995, pp. 363-86.

Scoring Key
To calculate your score, add up your responses to the six items.

Analysis and Interpretation
Not everyone is motivated to perform managerial functions. This instrument taps six components that have been found to be related to managerial success, especially in larger organizations. These are a favorable attitude toward authority; a desire to compete; a desire to exercise power; assertiveness; desire for a distinctive position; and a willingness to engage in repetitive tasks.

Scores on this instrument will range between 6 and 42. Arbitrary cut-offs suggest that scores of 6-18 indicate low motivation to manage; 19-29 is moderate motivation; and 30 and above as high motivation to manage.

What meaning can you draw from your score? It provides you with an idea of how comfortable you would be doing managerial activities. Note, however, that this instrument emphasizes tasks associated with managing in larger and more bureaucratic organizations. A low or moderate score may indicate that you're more suited to managing in a small firm, an organic organization, or in entrepreneurial situations.

III.B.5: Am I Well-Suited for a Career as a Global Manager?

Instrument

Indicate the extent to which you agree or disagree with each of the 14 statements in terms of how well they describe you. Use the following rating scale for your responses:

        1 = Very strongly disagree
        2 = Strongly disagree
        3 = Disagree
        4 = Neither agree or disagree
        5 = Agree
        6 = Strongly agree
        7 = Very strongly agree

1. When working with people from other cultures,
    I work hard to understand their perspectives.   1   2   3   4   5   6   7
2. I have a solid understanding of my organization's
    products and services.   1   2   3   4   5   6   7
3. I am willing to take a stand on issues.   1   2   3   4   5   6   7
4. I have a special talent for dealing with people.   1   2   3   4   5   6   7
5. I can be depended on to tell the truth regardless
    of circumstances.   1   2   3   4   5   6   7
6. I am good at identifying the most important part
    of a complex problem or issue.   1   2   3   4   5   6   7
7. I clearly demonstrate commitment to seeing
    the organization succeed.   1   2   3   4   5   6   7
8. I take personal as well as business risks.   1   2   3   4   5   6   7
9. I have changed as a result of feedback from others.   1   2   3   4   5   6   7
10. I enjoy the challenge of working in countries
    other than my own.   1   2   3   4   5   6   7
11. I take advantage of opportunities to do new things.   1   2   3   4   5   6   7
12. I find criticism hard to take.   1   2   3   4   5   6   7
13. I seek feedback even when others are
    reluctant to give it.   1   2   3   4   5   6   7
14. I don't get so invested in things that I cannot
    change when something doesn't work.   1   2   3   4   5   6   7

Source: Adapted from G.M. Spreitzer, M.W. McCall Jr., and J.D. Mahoney, "Early Identification of International Executive Potential," *Journal of Applied Psychology*, February 1997, pp. 6-29.

Scoring Key

To calculate your score, add up all your responses, except reverse your score for item 12.

Analysis and Interpretation

This instrument has been designed to tap dimensions associated with success as an international executive. These include general intelligence, business knowledge, interpersonal skills, commitment, courage, cross-cultural competencies, and the ability to learn from experience.

Total scores will fall between 14 and 98. The higher your score, the greater your potential for success as an international manager. While the authors of this instrument provided no specific cutoffs, it seems reasonable to assume that scores of 70 or higher indicate relatively strong potential for success in a global management position.

In today's global economy, being a manager often means being a *global* manager. But, unfortunately, not all managers are able to transfer their skills smoothly from domestic environments to global ones. Your results here can help you to assess whether your skills align with those needed to succeed as an international manager.

III.C.1: How Well Do I Respond to Turbulent Change?

Instrument

Listed to the right are a set of statements describing characteristics in a managerial job. If your job had these features, how would you react to them? Use the following rating scale for your answers:

        1 = This feature would be very unpleasant for me
        2 = This feature would be somewhat unpleasant for me
        3 = I'd have no reaction to this feature one way or another; or it would
                be about equally enjoyable and unpleasant
        4 = This would be enjoyable and acceptable most of the time
        5 = I would enjoy this very much; it's completely acceptable

1. I regularly spend 30 to 40 percent of my time in meetings.	1	2	3	4	5
2. A year and a half ago, my job did not exist, and I have been essentially inventing it as I go along.	1	2	3	4	5
3. The responsibilities I either assume or am assigned consistently exceed the authority I have for discharging them.	1	2	3	4	5
4. I am a member of a team and I have no more authority than anyone else on the team.	1	2	3	4	5
5. At any given moment in my job, I have on the average about a dozen phone calls or e-mails to be returned.	1	2	3	4	5
6. My job performance is evaluated by not only my boss, but also by my peers and subordinates.	1	2	3	4	5
7. About three weeks a year of formal management training is needed in my job just to stay current.	1	2	3	4	5
8. My job consistently brings me into close working contact at a professional level with people of many races, ethnic groups, and nationalities and of both sexes.	1	2	3	4	5
9. For many of my work colleagues, English is their second language.	1	2	3	4	5
10. My boss is from Germany and has only been in this country for six months.	1	2	3	4	5
11. There is no objective way to measure my effectiveness.	1	2	3	4	5
12. I report to three different bosses for different aspects of my job, and each has an equal say in my performance appraisal.	1	2	3	4	5
13. On average, about a third of my time is spent dealing with unexpected emergencies that force all scheduled work to be postponed.	1	2	3	4	5

14. On average, I spend about a week every month
    out of town on business.   1   2   3   4   5

15. I frequently have to work until 8p.m. to get my
    day's work completed.   1   2   3   4   5

16. When I have a meeting of the people who report
    to me, at least one or two will participate by
    phone or electronic conferencing.   1   2   3   4   5

17. The college degree I earned in preparation for
    this type of work is now obsolete, and I
    probably should go back for another degree.   1   2   3   4   5

18. My job requires me to absorb 100-to-200 pages
    per week of technical materials.   1   2   3   4   5

19. My department is so interdependent with several
    other departments in the organization that
    all distinctions about which departments are
    responsible for which tasks are quite arbitrary.   1   2   3   4   5

20. I am unlikely to get a promotion anytime in the
    near future.   1   2   3   4   5

21. There is no clear career path for me in this job
    and organization.   1   2   3   4   5

22. During the period of my employment here, either
    the entire organization or the division I worked
    in has been reorganized every year or so.   1   2   3   4   5

23. While I have many ideas about how to make things
    work better, I have no direct influence on either
    the business policies or the personnel policies
    that govern my division.   1   2   3   4   5

24. My organization is a defendant in an antitrust
    suit, and if the case comes to trial, I will probably
    have to testify about some decisions that were
    made a few years ago.   1   2   3   4   5

25. Sophisticated new technological equipment and
    software is continually being introduced into
    my division, necessitating constant learning
    on my part.   1   2   3   4   5

26. The computer I have in my office can be monitored
    by my bosses without my knowledge.   1   2   3   4   5

Source: Adapted from P.B. Vaill, *Managing as a Performing Art: New Ideas for a World of Chaotic Change* (San Francisco: Jossey-Bass, 1989), pp. 8-9.

Scoring Key
To calculate your tolerance of change score, add up your responses to the 26 questions.

Analysis and Interpretation

This instrument describes a number of characteristics of the changing workplace. The higher your score, the more comfortable you are with change.

The author of this instrument suggests an "average" score to be around 78. If you scored over 100, you seem to be accepting the "new" workplace fairly well. If your score was below 70, you're likely to find the manager's job in the 21st century to be unpleasant if not overwhelming.

III.C.2: How Stressful Is My Life?

Instrument

Review the following list of life events. Identify those that you have experienced in the last 12 months.

Life Event	Mean Value
1. Death of spouse	100
2. Divorce	73
3. Marital separation from mate	65
4. Detention in jail or other institution	63
5. Death of a close family member	63
6. Major personal injury or illness	53
7. Marriage	50
8. Being fired from job	47
9. Marital reconciliation with mate	45
10. Retirement from work	45
11. Major change in health or behavior of a family member	44
12. Pregnancy	40
13. Sexual difficulties	39
14. Gaining a new family member	39
15. Major business readjustment (merger, reorganization, bankruptcy, etc.)	39
16. Major change in financial state (positive or negative)	38
17. Death of a close friend	37
18. Changing to a different line of work	36
19. Major change in the number of arguments with spouse	35
20. Taking out a mortgage or loan for a major purchase (home, business, etc.)	31
21. Foreclosure on a mortgage or loan	30
22. Major change in responsibilities at work (promotion, demotion, transfer)	29
23. Son or daughter leaving home	29
24. In-law troubles	29
25. Outstanding personal achievement	28
26. Spouse beginning or ceasing work	26
27. Beginning or ceasing formal schooling	26
28. Major change in living conditions (building new house, remodeling, deterioration of neighborhood)	25
29. Revision of personal habits	24
30. Troubles with the boss	23
31. Major change in working hours or conditions	20
32. Change in residence	20
33. Changing to a new school	20
34. Major change in usual type and/or amount of recreation	19
35. Major change in church activities	19

36. Major change in social activities   18
37. Taking out a loan for a lesser purchase (car, TV, etc.)   17
38. Major change in sleeping habits.   16
39. Major change in number of family get-togethers   15
40. Major change in eating habits   15
41. Vacation   13
42. Christmas   12
43. Minor violation of the law (traffic tickets, disturbing
    the peace, etc.)   11

Source: T.H. Holmes and R.H. Rahe, "The Social Readjustment Rating Scale," *Journal of Psychometric Research*, 1967, pp. 213-18.

Scoring Key
To calculate your score, add up the mean values for the events that you've experienced in the past year.

Analysis and Interpretation
Life change events build up and create stress. This instrument weighs the events you've experienced in the past year in terms of their potential to create stress-induced illnesses or injuries during the next two-year period. Notice that positive events (marriage, a promotion, an inheritance) as well as negative ones can create stress.

    A cumulative score of 150 or less indicates a low susceptibility to stress-induced illnesses or injuries. A score of 151 to 300 indicate a 35 to 50 percent probability of stress related health changes in the next two-year period. And scores of over 300 indicate an 80 percent chance of stress-induced health changes.

    This instrument dramatizes that changes accumulate and, if they accumulate too much, they can overtake your body's ability to adjust. Some events are uncontrollable by you. Others, however, are within your control. Don't try to undertake too much change too fast. Of course, different personality types handle stress differently. Hardy-types seem to do better at dealing with change and stress. These are people who believe they can control the events they encounter, are extremely committed to the activities in their lives, and who treat change in their lives as a challenge. If you're a hardy-type, a high score on this instrument may not lead to negative health changes.

III.C.3: Am I Burned Out?

Instrument
Respond to each of the 21 items using the following scale:

        1 = Never
        2 = Once in a while
        3 = Rarely
        4 = Sometimes
        5 = Often
        6 = Usually
        7 = Always

How often do you have any of the following experiences?

1. Being tired	1	2	3	4	5	6	7
2. Feeling depressed	1	2	3	4	5	6	7
3. Having a good day	1	2	3	4	5	6	7
4. Being physically exhausted	1	2	3	4	5	6	7
5. Being emotionally exhausted	1	2	3	4	5	6	7
6. Being happy	1	2	3	4	5	6	7
7. Being "wiped out"	1	2	3	4	5	6	7
8. "Can't take it anymore"	1	2	3	4	5	6	7
9. Being unhappy	1	2	3	4	5	6	7
10. Feeling run-down	1	2	3	4	5	6	7
11. Feeling trapped	1	2	3	4	5	6	7
12. Feeling worthless	1	2	3	4	5	6	7
13. Being weary	1	2	3	4	5	6	7
14. Being troubled	1	2	3	4	5	6	7
15. Feeling disillusioned and resentful	1	2	3	4	5	6	7
16. Being weak and susceptible to illness	1	2	3	4	5	6	7
17. Feeling hopeless	1	2	3	4	5	6	7
18. Feeling rejected	1	2	3	4	5	6	7
19. Feeling optimistic	1	2	3	4	5	6	7
20. Feeling energetic	1	2	3	4	5	6	7
21. Feeling anxious	1	2	3	4	5	6	7

Source: A. Pines and E. Aronson, "Why Managers Burn Out," *Sales & Marketing Management*, February 1989, p. 38.

Scoring Key
To calculate your burnout score, add up your score for items 3, 6, 19, and 20. Then subtract that total from 32. To this number, add your direct scores for the remaining 17 items. Finally, divide this combined number by 21.

Analysis and Interpretation
Burnout is the exhibiting of chronic and long-term stress. This instrument was designed to provide you insights into whether you're suffering from burnout.

Your burnout score will lie somewhere between 1 and 7. The higher your number, the closer you are to burnout. The authors claim that scores below 3 indicate few signs of burnout. Scores between 3 and 4 suggest the need to examine your work life and reevaluate priorities with the intent of making changes. If your score is higher than 4, you are experiencing a number of signs associated with burnout. You need to take some action to address your problems. Scores above 5 indicate an acute state, requiring immediate professional attention.

What can you do if you're showing serious signs of burnout? The place to begin might be reading B. Potter and P. Frank, *Overcoming Job Burnout: How to Renew Enthusiasm for Work, 2/e* (Ronin, 1998) or S. Cartwright and C.L. Cooper, *Managing Workplace Stress* (Sage, 1997).

IV.A.1: Am I a Narcissist?

Instrument
For each of the following statements, indicate with a "yes" or a "no" whether you believe that statement describes you.

0=no
1=yes

1. I have a natural talent for influencing people.
2. I really like to be the center of attention.
3. I see myself as a good leader.
4. I like to look at myself in the mirror.
5. I am an extraordinary person.
6. I have good taste when it comes to beauty.
7. I usually dominate any conversation.
8. Everybody likes to hear my stories.
9. I can read people like a book.
10. I will never be satisfied until I get all that I deserve.
11. I am envious of other people's good fortune.
12. I am more capable than other people.

_____

Source: Adapted from: R. A. Emmons, "Narcissism: Theory and Measurement," *Journal of Personality and Social Psychology,* 1987, 52, pp. 11-17. This measure is an abridged version of the Narcissistic Personality Inventory (NPI; Raskin & Hall, 1979):
R. Raskin, and C. S. Hall, "A Narcissistic Personality Inventory," *Psychological Reports,* 1979, 45, p. 590.

Scoring Key
To score the measure, compute the number of "yes" responses. Scores will range from zero to 12.

Analysis and Interpretation
This measure assesses narcissistic personality. Narcissism is defined as a grandiose sense of self-importance. Narcissists believe that anything they do will be successful, believe they are special and unique, possess a strong sense of entitlement, like to be admired by others, and in general are arrogant and conceited. Scores on this scale range from zero to 12, with higher scores indicating a more narcissistic personality.

Although narcissism has been studied in psychology for decades, research is only beginning to examine the effects of narcissism in the workplace. Recent research has found a number of negative work outcomes associated with narcissism. Employees who are narcissistic are judged by their coworkers to exhibit fewer leadership behaviors, fewer positive, helpful behaviors, and more negative, deviant behaviors. Interestingly, narcissists don't perceive themselves that way – they believe that they are strong, effective leaders.

Don't confuse narcissism with self-esteem. Though narcissism and self-esteem are positively related, narcissism doesn't simply reflect extremely high self-esteem. Having a positive view of oneself is one thing (and can be beneficial); viewing oneself as superior to others and possessing exploitative tendencies is another (and can be detrimental). In today's organizations, where teams are increasingly being used to accomplish work, narcissists may be especially harmful, as their highly competitive tendencies get in the way of cooperation and teamwork.

IV.A.2: Am I A Deliberate Decision-Maker?

Instrument
Indicate to what extent the following statements describe you when you make decisions.

1=to a very little extent
2=to a little extent
3=somewhat
4=to a large extent
5=to a very large extent

1. I jump into things without thinking.
2. I make rash decisions.
3. I like to act on a whim.
4. I rush into things.
5. I don't know why I do some of the things I do.
6. I act quickly without thinking.
7. I choose my words with care.

_____

Source: *Based on*: L. R. Goldberg, J. A. Johnson, H. W. Eber, R. Hogan, M. C. Ashton, C. R. Cloninger, and H. G. Gough, "The International Personality Item Pool and the Future of Public-Domain Personality Measures," *Journal of Research in Personality,* 2006, 40, 84-96.

Scoring Key
To score the measure, first reverse-code items 1, 2, 3, 4, 5, and 6 so that 1=5, 2=4, 3=3, 4=2, and 5=1. Then, compute the sum of the 7 items. Scores will range from 7 to 35.

Analysis and Interpretation
People differ in how they make decisions. Some people prefer to collect information, carefully weigh alternatives, and then select the best option, while others prefer to make a choice as quickly as possible.

This scale assesses how deliberate you are when making decisions. If you scored at or above 28, you tend to be quite deliberate. If you scored at or below 14, you tend to be rash. Scores between 14 and 27 reveal a more blended style of decision making.

How should decisions be made? The rational model states that individuals should define the problem, identify what criteria are relevant to making the decision and weigh those criteria according to importance, develop alternatives, and finally evaluate and select the best alternative. Though this sounds like an arduous process, research has shown that the rational model tends to result in better decisions.

If you tend to make decisions on a whim, you may want to be especially careful in auction settings, such as those found on the Web site eBay. The time pressures involved, along with the emotional arousal that comes with bidding, can result in "auction fever" and suboptimal decisions. Put simply, if you make quick, impulsive decisions, you may pay more than you should have.

Interestingly, personality is related to a person's decision-making style. Individuals who are deliberate and decisive tend to be high in emotional stability and high in conscientiousness, while individuals who are more impulsive tend to be low on these two traits. Thus, while your decision-making style is likely to be somewhat stable, following the rational model should help you to avoid making rash decisions.

IV.A.3: How Confident Am I in My Abilities to Succeed?

Instrument
Indicate the extent to which you agree or disagree with each of the following statements using the scale below.

1=strongly disagree
2=disagree
3=neutral
4=agree
5=strongly agree

1. I am strong enough to overcome life's struggles.
2. At root, I am a weak person.
3. I can handle the situations that life brings.
4. I usually feel that I am an unsuccessful person.
5. I often feel that there is nothing that I can do well.
6. I feel competent to deal effectively with the real world.
7. I often feel like a failure.
8. I usually feel I can handle the typical problems that come up in life.

Source: T. A. Judge, E. A. Locke, C. C. Durham, and A. N. Kluger, "Dispositional Effects on Job and Life Satisfaction: The Role of Core Evaluations," *Journal of Applied Psychology*, 1998, 83, pp. 17-34.

Scoring Key
To score the measure, first reverse-code items 2, 4, 5, and 7 so that 1=5, 2=4, 3=3, 4=2, and 5=1. Then, compute the sum of the 8 items. Scores will range from 8 to 40.

Analysis and Interpretation
Confidence has an influence on many things we do. Your score on this measure can range from 8 to 40; the higher your score, the more confidence you have in yourself to be successful.

People who are confident have high self-efficacy that generalizes across a variety of situations. They believe that they have the capability to mobilize the motivation and resources required to perform successfully on different tasks they encounter. Ultimately, this confidence translates into better performance. Why? One reason is that efficacious individuals set more goals for themselves, are more committed to their goals, and even persist in achieving their goals in the face of failure. In fact, when individuals who are confident about themselves are given negative feedback (say, by a supervisor), they respond by *increasing* their effort and motivation. Perhaps not surprisingly, individuals with such positive self-concepts are more satisfied with their jobs and obtain higher levels of career success.

If you don't have a great deal of confidence in yourself, there are several ways to increase it. One way is to simply gain experience with tasks that you are less confident about. Another way is to watch someone else, such as a friend, perform the task. For example, if you don't have confidence in your ability to hit a tennis ball, first observing someone else do it is likely to boost your confidence. Finally, being persuaded by someone else that you can do something (think motivational speaker) helps to increase the efficacy of individuals to perform a given task.

IV.A.4: How Spiritual Am I?

Instrument
Using the scale below, indicate the extent to which you agree or disagree with each of the following statements.

1=strongly disagree
2=disagree
3=neutral
4=agree
5=strongly agree

1. I believe in a universal power or God.
2. I am a spiritual person.
3. I keep my faith even during hard times.
4. I have spent at least 30 minutes in the last 24 hours in prayer or meditation.
5. I am who I am because of my faith.
6. I believe that each person has a purpose in life.
7. I know that my beliefs make my life important.
8. I do not practice any religion.

Source: L. R. Goldberg, J. A. Johnson, H. W. Eber, R. Hogan, M. C. Ashton, C. R. Cloninger, and H. G. Gough, "The International Personality Item Pool and the Future of Public-Domain Personality Measures," *Journal of Research in Personality,* 2006, 40, 84-96.

Scoring Key
To score the measure, first reverse-code item 8 so that 1=5, 2=4, 3=3, 4=2, and 5=1. Then, compute the sum of the 8 items. Scores will range from 8 to 40.

Analysis and Interpretation
Although early views of organizations as rational systems disregarded the inner lives of employees, contemporary views now recognize that the inner lives of employees can have a major influence on their experiences at work. This scale measures how spiritual you perceive yourself to be. Your score on this measure can range from 8 to 40; the higher the score, the more spiritual you are, believing that life has a higher meaning and purpose and transcends that which we can observe directly.

Because the potential importance of spirituality in the workplace has only recently been recognized, little is known about how spirituality affects individuals at work. Some research has indicated that companies that provide opportunities for employees to develop spiritually perform better than those that do not. Culture is important, as companies without a supportive culture may result in employee reluctance to express their spirituality. In addition, some researchers have suggested that spiritual leaders are better able to motivate their followers than non-spiritual leaders. They argue that spiritual leaders are better able to create a vision that results in followers experiencing a greater sense of meaning at work. In addition, spiritual leaders are proposed to show greater concern and empathy, which makes followers feel better understood and appreciated. Thus, although we are gaining a better understanding of spirituality in the workplace, much more research is needed.

IV.B.1: Am I Engaged?

Instrument
Indicate the extent to which you agree or disagree with each of the following items using the scale below.

1=strongly disagree
2=agree
3=neutral
4=agree
5=strongly agree

13. When I get up in the morning, I feel like going to class.
14. As far as my studies are concerned, I always persevere, even when things do not go well.
15. I can continue to study for very long periods at a time.
16. My study inspires me.
17. I am enthusiastic about my studies.
18. I find my studies full of meaning and purpose.
19. When I am studying, I forget everything else around me.
20. I am immersed in my studies.
21. I feel happy when I am studying intensely.

_____

Source: Adapted from: W. B. Schaufeli, M. Salanova, V. Gonzalez-Roma, and A. B. Bakker, "The Measurement of Engagement and Burnout: A Two-Sample Confirmatory Factor Analytic Approach," *Journal of Happiness Studies,* 2002, 3, pp. 71-92.

Scoring Key
To score the measure, compute the sum of the nine items. Scores will range from nine to 45.

Analysis and Interpretation
This scale measures work engagement, which is defined as a persisting, positive state of motivation and fulfillment. Your score on this measure can range from 9 to 45; the higher your score, the more engaged you are. Individuals who are engaged are willing to devote considerable time to their work, are dedicated and persist in the face of obstacles, feel inspired by and proud of their work, and become immersed and absorbed while performing their work.

High engagement thus sounds like a good thing to have. Not surprisingly, this "super motivation" has been linked to lots of positive outcomes in organizations. Employees who are engaged are more satisfied with and committed to their jobs, less absent, and less likely to quit than employees who are not engaged. Engaged employees also perform better and help others more than less engaged employees.

There are lots of reasons why some individuals are more engaged than others. For example, people find some jobs and tasks to be more engaging than others, such as those with a lot of variety and autonomy (see Job Characteristics Theory). If you find yourself feeling disengaged, try setting some specific but challenging goals for yourself. Also, following a tough, stressful day at school or at work, take some leisurely time off – the recovery is likely to make you more engaged the next day.

IV.C.1: What's My Attitude Toward Older People?

Instrument
Below is a list of adjectives. Consider each adjective, and then indicate the extent to which you agree or disagree with whether it describes older people in general.

1=strongly disagree
2=agree
3=neutral
4=agree
5=strongly agree

22. Forgetful
23. Slow thinking
24. Incapable of handling job
25. Bitter
26. Set in ways
27. Wise
28. Active
29. Generous
30. Know a great deal
31. Interesting

_____

Source: *Based on*: D. F. Schmidt, and S. M. Boland, "Structure of Perceptions of Older Adults: Evidence for Multiple Stereotypes," *Psychology and Aging,* 1986, 3, pp. 255-260.

Scoring Key
To score the measure, first reverse-code items 1, 2, 3, 4, and 5 so that 1=5, 2=4, 3=3, 4=2, and 5=1. Then, compute the sum of the 10 items. Scores will range from 10 to 50.

Analysis and Interpretation
This scale assesses the degree to which you hold positive or negative attitudes toward older people. Your score will range from 10 to 50, with lower scores indicating more negative attitudes and higher scores indicating more positive attitudes.

One thing is certain about the workforce: it is growing older. By 2010, the average age of the workforce is expected to be 41. In addition, employees 50 and older are expected to outnumber those 49 and younger by around 4 to 1 by 2012. Given that it's very likely that many of your work colleagues will be older individuals, the attitudes that you hold toward them are important to consider.

Contrary to the sometimes negative stereotypes held toward older employees (e.g., they aren't motivated to learn new things, they are less capable than younger employees, and they are difficult to work with), companies are discovering the benefits of employing older adults. Older employees are absent less than younger employees, and their turnover rates are lower. In addition, the accumulated work experience of older workers can boost performance levels. In fact, some companies, such as Home Depot, are hiring older workers who have retired from their former jobs because of the benefits they bring.

Holding negative attitudes toward older employees may lead to more interpersonal conflicts and frustration, which can make working together difficult. In addition,
people who hold negative attitudes may miss out on valuable mentoring that older workers can provide. If this measure reveals a negative attitude, try considering the advantages that older employees bring to the workplace.

IV.C.2: What Are My Gender Role Perceptions?

Instrument
For each of the following statements, indicate your extent of agreement or disagreement using the scale below.

1=strongly disagree
2=disagree
3=agree
4=strongly agree

1. A woman's place is in the home, not the office or shop.
2. A wife with a family has no time for outside employment.
3. A working wife feels more useful than one who doesn't hold a job.
4. Employment of wives leads to more juvenile delinquency.
5. Employment of both parents is necessary to keep up with the high cost of living.
6. It is much better for everyone concerned if the man is the achiever outside the home and the woman takes care of the home and family.
7. Men should share the work around the house with women, such as doing dishes, cleaning, and so forth.
8. Women are much happier if they stay home and take care of children.

Source: Bureau of Labor Statistics

Scoring Key
To score the measure, first reverse-code items 3, 5, and 7 so that 1=4, 2=3, 3=2, and 4=1. Then, compute the sum of the 8 items. Scores will range from 8 to 32.

Analysis and Interpretation
These items measure how traditional your attitudes are toward women participating in the workforce. One of the most dramatic changes in the workforce over the past several decades has been the inclusion of women. In 1970, around 43% of women participated in the workforce; in 2004, that number increased to 59%. Given that women currently outnumber men on college campuses throughout the United States, these numbers are expected to rise. Thus, women are continuing to move away from their traditional role as homemaker.

If you scored above 23, you hold more traditional views toward women and feel that their place is in the home. Scores below 17 indicate less traditional views toward women; you feel that both men and women should be able to participate in the workforce. Scores between 17 and 23 indicate neither traditional nor non-traditional views.

Increasingly, attitudes toward women are becoming less traditional, especially among younger people. In a national survey of over 7,600 individuals in their late 40s, around 11% strongly agreed with the traditional statements (e.g., "Women are much happier if they stay home and take care of children"), and 29% indicated that they agreed with the statements. Still, among this age group, over half of the respondents endorsed the less traditional statements. With the increasing participation of women in the labor force, holding a more traditional view of women may make it more difficult to get along with coworkers.

IV.D.1: How Are You Feeling Right Now?

Instrument
Below are a number of adjectives that describe different emotions you may be feeling. Indicate the extent to which you are feeling each emotion right now.

1=very slightly or not at all
2=a little
3=moderately
4=quite a bit
5=very much

32. Happy
33. Cheerful
34. Delighted
35. Excited
36. Enthusiastic
37. Distressed
38. Angry
39. Fearful
40. Sad
41. Ashamed

_____

Source: Tim Judge. With permission.

Scoring Key
To score the measure, first reverse-code items 6, 7, 8, 9, and 10 so that 1=5, 2=4, 3=3, 4=2, and 5=1. Then, compute the sum of the 10 items. Scores will range from 10 to 50.

Analysis and Interpretation
This scale measures whether you are currently experiencing positive or negative emotions. Your score on this measure can range from 10 to 50, with higher numbers indicating that you are experiencing more positive emotions and lower numbers indicating that you are experiencing more negative emotions. If you took some of the other measures in this self-assessment library (such as those on personality and attitudes) more than once, your scores would probably be similar. In contrast, your scores on this measure may vary quite a bit from one day to the next. This is because the emotions we feel change regularly; we might feel happy or excited at one moment but sad or angry the next.

The emotions we experience have an influence on our behavior in organizations. In general, people and organizations tend to benefit from positive emotions. When we experience positive emotions, we tend to be more creative, more satisfied with our jobs, and more willing to help our coworkers. In contrast, when we experience negative emotions, we tend to be less motivated, more likely to find ourselves in interpersonal conflicts, and more likely to engage in deviant workplace behaviors. Interestingly, the emotions we experience can affect others too. Both positive and negative emotions can be contagious. So, displaying positive emotions around others can put those others in a good mood, while displaying negative emotions around others can put those others in a bad mood. Finally, research has shown that our personalities influence the emotions we regularly experience. While extraverted people tend to experience more positive emotions, neurotic people tend to display more negative emotions, even if they are exposed to the same event.

IV.D.2: What's My Affect Intensity?

Instrument
Indicate the extent to which you agree or disagree with each of the following statements using the response scale below.

1=strongly disagree
2=agree
3=neutral
4=agree
5=strongly agree

1. I experience my emotions intensely.
2. I feel others' emotions.
3. I am passionate about causes.
4. I enjoy examining myself and my life.
5. I try to understand myself.
6. I seldom get emotional.
7. I am not easily affected by my emotions.
8. I rarely notice my emotional reactions.
9. I experience very few emotional highs and lows.
10. I don't understand people who get emotional.

Source: L. R. Goldberg, J. A. Johnson, H. W. Eber, R. Hogan, M. C. Ashton, C. R. Cloninger, and H. G. Gough, "The International Personality Item Pool and the Future of Public-Domain Personality Measures," *Journal of Research in Personality,* 2006, 40, 84-96.

Scoring Key
To score the measure, first reverse-code items 6, 7, 8, 9, and 10 so that 1=5, 2=4, 3=3, 4=2, and 5=1. Then, compute the sum of the 10 items. Scores will range from 10 to 50.

Analysis and Interpretation
People differ in the strength with which they experience their emotions. Some individuals experience and display their emotions intensely, while others experience and display their emotions mildly. For example, while watching a sad movie, one person may burst into tears, while another person may not react at all. This scale assesses your emotional intensity. You score can range from 10 to 50; the higher the score, the more emotionally intense you are.

Some individuals tend to be more emotionally intense than others. For example, neurotic individuals tend to have higher levels of emotional intensity than emotionally stable individuals; women tend to experience their emotions more intensely than men, and Americans tend to be higher in emotional intensity than Chinese.

Your level of emotional intensity can have implications at work. Jobs place different demands on individuals' emotions and their expression of those emotions. In some cases, high emotional intensity is required. Trial lawyers, actors, and sports commentators all need to display their emotions strongly or weakly depending on the circumstances. In contrast, air traffic controllers and judges are typically required to keep their emotions in check. Whether the emotion is positive or negative makes a difference too. Those in the service industry are often required to display high levels of positive emotions during encounters with customers, but to not display negative emotions. Often, attempting to display (or not display) an emotion contrary to what one is currently feeling can be stressful and taxing and may result in feelings of burnout.

IV.E.1: What's My Attitude Toward Working in Groups?

Instrument
Using the scale below, indicate the extent to which you agree or disagree with each of the following statements about your feelings toward working in groups or teams.

1=strongly disagree
2=disagree
3=neutral
4=agree
5=strongly agree

1. I don't miss group meetings or team practices.
2. I enjoy being part of a group.
3. I support my teammates or fellow group members.
4. I feel I must respect the decisions made by my group.
5. I am not good at working with a group.
6. I prefer to do everything alone.
7. I work best when I am alone.
8. I keep to myself.
9. I don't think it's important to socialize with others.

_____

Source: L. R. Goldberg, J. A. Johnson, H. W. Eber, R. Hogan, M. C. Ashton, C. R. Cloninger, and H. G. Gough, "The International Personality Item Pool and the Future of Public-Domain Personality Measures," _Journal of Research in Personality,_ 2006, 40, 84-96.

Scoring Key
To score the measure, first reverse-code items 5, 6, 7, 8, and 9 so that 1=5, 2=4, 3=3, 4=2, and 5=1. Then, compute the sum of the 9 items. Scores will range from 9 to 45.

Analysis and Interpretation
One thing is certain about organizations these days: more and more work is being performed by groups and teams. In fact, over 80% of Fortune 500 companies use teams in some way to accomplish work. So, it's quite likely that you'll be part of a team at some point if you have not already.

This measure assesses your attitudes toward working in groups. Scores at or above 36 indicate that you enjoy working in groups and that you are a "team player." Scores at or below 18 indicate the opposite – that you prefer to work alone and do not enjoy being part of a team. Scores between 18 and 36 indicate no particular strong feelings either way.

Teams comprised of members who enjoy being part of a group can be quite effective. However, research has indicated that as little as one person with a negative attitude toward working in groups can hurt team performance. In other words, "one bad apple can spoil the barrel." Why? Team members with negative attitudes can increase interpersonal conflict among group members, harming cohesiveness specifically and team processes more generally. Team morale and satisfaction is lowered, and performance ultimately declines.

If you scored low on this measure and find yourself on a group or team at some point, try to see the benefits of teamwork. Not only is work shared among individuals, but teams also can facilitate feelings of inclusion and camaraderie among team members. Remember to be patient, however, although teams often outperform individuals working by themselves (especially on complex tasks that require multiple skills and experience), they tend to take longer to reach decisions.

IV.E.2: What Is My Team Efficacy?

Instrument
Reflecting on your past experience in all of the teams that you have been on, please answer the following questions regarding the extent to which you personally feel capable of exhibiting the below behaviors.

1=not at all
2=barely
3=a little
4=somewhat
5=fairly
6=quite a bit
7=very much so

1. Set time deadlines for achieving tasks.
2. Take steps to ensure everyone participates in group discussions.
3. Take the group's ideas and develop specific plans of action.
4. Make correct judgments about connections in complex situations.
5. Participate in developing strategies to achieve team goals.
6. Remind other team members of the team's goal.
7. Draw team members into discussions that are relevant to achieving the goal.
8. Ignore or discourage off-topic conversations.
9. Steer team members towards on-topic conversations.
10. Address conflict immediately by raising it for discussion with other team members.
11. Try to calm down team members that are in conflict.
12. Assume leadership.

Source: K. Tasa, S. Taggar, and G. H. Seijts, "The Development of Collective Efficacy in Teams: A Multilevel and Longitudinal Perspective," *Journal of Applied Psychology* (Jan 2007), pp. 17-27.

Scoring Key
To score the measure, compute the average (sum each response and divide by 12). Scores will range from 1 to 7.

Analysis and Interpretation
When working in teams, people differ in their confidence of the team's capability to perform tasks successfully. This is referred to as team efficacy.

Scores on this measure range from 1 to 7, and higher scores indicate greater confidence in a team's ability to perform well. Team efficacy influences lots of team dynamics, including what team members choose to do with their time, how much effort they expend on a given task, and how much they persist in the face of failure. Not surprisingly, high team efficacy is associated with greater motivation and team effectiveness. Another interesting finding on team efficacy is that team efficacy matters more to team performance when team members are highly interdependent, meaning that they must communicate and share resources with one another in order to complete the task at hand.

If you score low on this measure, you may interact in negative ways with your teammates, changing the team's confidence over time. Downward "spirals" may ensue, as lower team efficacy results in lower team performance, which then results in even lower team efficacy, and so forth.

The good news is that several things have been shown to increase team efficacy. Previous successes, even if they are small, increase team efficacy. In addition, verbal persuasion by team members increases team efficacy. The end result may be upward rather than downward performance spirals!

IV.E.3: Am I a Gossip?

Instrument

Rate the extent to which you agree or disagree with each of the items below, using the following scale.

1=disagree strongly
2=disagree
3=neutral
4=agree
5=agree strongly

1. I mind my own business instead of gossiping.
2. I love to know what is going on in people's lives.
3. I like to share what I hear.
4. It is fun to talk about other people.
5. Gossiping is a great way to pass time.
6. Gossip is a good ice-breaker.
7. One cannot trust gossip.
8. I have never known gossip to be helpful.
9. Gossip is often true.
10. One should never mention rumors even if true.
11. Rumors are hardly ever true.
12. It is wrong to talk about others.

_____

Source: J. A. Litman, and M. V. Pezzo, "Individual Differences in Attitudes Towards Gossip," *Personality and Individual Differences* (March 2005), pp. 963-980.

Scoring Key

To score the measure, first reverse-code items 1, 7, 8, 10, 11, 12 so that 1=5, 2=4, 3=3, 4=2, and 5=1. Then, compute the sum of the 12 items. Scores will range from 12 to 60.

Analysis and Interpretation

Gossip refers to informal and evaluative talk among individuals about another person who usually is not present when the information is shared. Individuals differ in their attitudes towards gossip; some view gossip positively, while others view gossip negatively. Those who hold positive attitudes towards gossip feel that it is valuable for making friends and gathering information. Those who hold negative feelings towards gossip feel that it causes social problems and hurts others who are the targets of gossip.

This measure assesses whether you perceive gossip positively or negatively. Scores range from 12 to 60, with higher scores indicating more positive attitudes towards gossip. Higher scores indicate that you like to engage in and listen to gossip, and you also tend to believe gossip when you hear it.

Despite the often negative connotations that come with the term "gossip," gossip can be either negative or positive. Research has shown that positive gossip can enhance the gossip recipient's reputation, while negative gossip can harm it. The effects of gossip aren't just limited to the targets of gossip – those who initiate gossip (gossipers) tend to be viewed by others as sources of useful information. Gossipers may also be perceived by others as more powerful within organizations because they appear to be "in the loop" more and hold more information than others. However, this doesn't necessarily mean that you should gossip more about others. Too much gossip may irritate others. Also, in organizations, if gossip is perceived by others to not be credible, or if gossip is not relevant to work, then the reputation of the gossiper may decline.

IV.E.4: Am I an Ethical Leader?

Instrument
Using the response scale below, indicate when, in leadership positions, how likely you are to engage in the following behaviors.

1=highly unlikely
2=unlikely
3=slightly unlikely
4=neither likely nor unlikely
5=slightly likely
6=likely
7=highly likely

1. I listen to what others have to say.
2. I speak out when others violate ethical standards.
3. I conduct my personal life in an ethical manner.
4. I have the best interests of others in mind.
5. I make fair and balanced decisions.
6. I can be trusted.
7. I discuss business ethics or values with others.
8. I set an example of how to do things the right way in terms of ethics.
9. I define success not just by results but also the way that they are obtained.
10. When making decisions, I ask "what is the right thing to do?"

_____

Source: *Based on*: M. E. Brown, L. K. Treviño, and D. A. Harrison, "Ethical Leadership: A Social Learning Perspective for Construct Development and Testing," *Organizational Behavior and Human Decision Processes,* 2005, 97, pp. 117-134.

Scoring Key
To score the measure, compute the sum of the 10 items. Scores will range from 10 to 70.

Analysis and Interpretation
Ethical leaders demonstrate appropriate conduct through personal actions and interpersonal relationships, and they promote their conduct to their followers through communication, reinforcement, and decision making. This scale assesses the degree of ethical leadership you believe you possess. Although there are no cutoffs between being an ethical leader and an unethical leader, scores range from 10 to 70, and higher scores are preferred because they indicate higher levels of ethical leadership.

With recent ethical scandals in business, ethical leadership has become an important topic. Research has revealed numerous benefits of being an ethical leader. Not only are ethical leaders trusted more by their followers, but also their followers are more satisfied, more willing to give extra effort to their jobs, and more open to reporting problems and issues to management compared to followers of unethical leaders. Why are there so many positive effects on followers?

One reason is that ethical leaders are perceived as attractive and legitimate role models that followers try to emulate.

If you scored low on this scale, the good news is that ethical leaders can be developed to some degree. Having an ethical leader as a mentor, behaving in a fair and considerate manner toward others, and being honest with others are all ways in which individuals can be perceived by others as more ethical.

IV.E.5: What Is My LPC Score?

Instrument

Think of all the people with whom you have ever worked. From those people, select the coworker who you preferred the LEAST (the coworker with whom you had the most difficulty in getting a job done). Next, use the adjectives below to describe this person.

Unfriendly							Friendly
1	2	3	4	5	6	7	8

Insincere							Sincere
1	2	3	4	5	6	7	8

Distant							Close
1	2	3	4	5	6	7	8

Hostile							Supportive
1	2	3	4	5	6	7	8

Quarrelsome							Harmonious
1	2	3	4	5	6	7	8

Rejecting							Accepting
1	2	3	4	5	6	7	8

Cold							Warm
1	2	3	4	5	6	7	8

Inconsiderate							Considerate
1	2	3	4	5	6	7	8

Disagreeable							Agreeable
1	2	3	4	5	6	7	8

Tense							Relaxed
1	2	3	4	5	6	7	8

Nasty							Nice
1	2	3	4	5	6	7	8

Unpleasant							Pleasant
1	2	3	4	5	6	7	8

Boring							Interesting
1	2	3	4	5	6	7	8

Untrustworthy							Trustworthy
1	2	3	4	5	6	7	8

Backbiting							Loyal
1	2	3	4	5	6	7	8

Unkind							Kind
1	2	3	4	5	6	7	8

Source: Based on: F. E. Fiedler and J. E. Garcia, *New approaches to effective leadership: Cognitive resources and organizational performance,* 1987, New York: Wiley.

Scoring Key
To score the measure, compute the sum of the 16 items. Scores will range from 16 to 128.

Analysis and Interpretation
Fred Fiedler proposed an interesting way to determine people's leadership styles — by considering how they view the coworker with whom they enjoy working with the *least*. This *least preferred coworker scale* assesses your view. Scores range from 16 to 128. Scores above 90 indicate that your leadership style is relationship-oriented, meaning that, as a leader, you are primarily interested in developing and maintaining positive interpersonal relationships with followers. Scores below 54 indicate that your leadership style is task-oriented, meaning that, as a leader, you are primarily interested in generating the most productivity from your followers. Scores in between (54 to 90) indicate no particular leadership style.

Fiedler went one step further than characterizing individuals' leadership styles. He suggested that the effectiveness of one's leadership style depends on the situation in which the leader is placed. He described situations in terms of three dimensions:

1) Leader-member relations: The degree of confidence, trust, and respect members have in their leader.
2) Task structure: The degree to which the job assignments are structured vs. unstructured.
3) Position power: The degree of influence a leader has over power variables such as hiring, firing, discipline, promotions, and salary increases.

Fiedler suggested that leaders have more control over their followers when leader-member relations are good, tasks are highly structured, and position power is high. If you are a task-oriented leader, you're more likely to be successful under situations of high and low control. In contrast, if you are a relationship-oriented leader, you're more likely to be successful under situations of moderate control. Although complex, Fiedler's contingency model of leadership has received support.

IV.F.1: Is My Workplace Political?

Instrument
Think about the current place where you work. If you are not currently working, think about the place where you last worked. Next, indicate the extent to which you agree with each of the following statements.

1=disagree strongly
2=disagree
3=neutral
4=agree
5=agree strongly

1. People like to play politics at this organization.
2. Getting ahead in this organization is more about who you know, not how well you perform.
3. It is clear that a small number of individuals in this organization hold all the power.
4. People in this organization will stab others in the back just to get ahead.
5. The only person I can trust in this organization is myself.

_____

Source: Tim Judge. With permission.

Scoring Key
To score the measure, sum the 5 items. Scores will range from 5 to 25.

Analysis and Interpretation
Political behavior, defined as self-serving behavior not formally sanctioned by the organization, exists to some degree in virtually every organization. Some organizations are characterized by extreme levels of political activity, while others are less political. This scale assesses how political you perceive your workplace to be. Scores range from 5 to 25, with higher scores indicating greater political activity.

Although political behavior can sometimes be positive (especially for those who benefit from it!), mostly it is viewed negatively by employees. Specifically, highly political organizations are perceived by employees as stressful, creating day-to-day anxiety. As a result, organizations that are highly political tend to have higher levels of employee absenteeism, job dissatisfaction, and turnover.

Political behavior in organizations is more likely under certain conditions and with certain types of employees. When there are loose rules and regulations governing behavior, when uncertainty is high, and when resources are scare, politicking is more likely. Employees who have a high need for power, who are high self-monitors, and who believe they can control their environment (i.e., possess an internal locus of control), are more likely to engage in political activities. Moreover, political behavior in organizations can be self-reinforcing – if employees perceive that others get ahead through political means, they will be more likely to use political tactics themselves.

IV.F.2: Do I Like Bureaucracy?

Instrument
Indicate the extent to which you agree or disagree with each of the following statements using the response scale below.

1=strongly disagree
2=agree
3=neutral
4=agree
5=strongly agree

42. I love order and regularity.
43. I like to work according to a routine.
44. I respect authority.
45. I prefer to observe formalities.
46. I don't like the feeling of being directed or controlled.
47. I dislike routine.
48. I oppose authority.
49. I like to dispense with formalities.

Source: *Based on*: L. R. Goldberg, J. A. Johnson, H. W. Eber, R. Hogan, M. C. Ashton, C. R. Cloninger, and H. G. Gough, "The International Personality Item Pool and the Future of Public-Domain Personality Measures," *Journal of Research in Personality,* 2006, 40, 84-96.

Scoring Key
To score the measure, first reverse-code items 5, 6, 7, and 8 so that 1=5, 2=4, 3=3, 4=2, and 5=1. Then, compute the sum of the 8 items. Scores will range from 8 to 40.

Analysis and Interpretation
This instrument measures your preference for working in a bureaucratic organization. Bureaucratic organizations are characterized by a rigid, hierarchical structure with a high concentration of power at the top of the hierarchy. Work in bureaucratic organizations tends to be highly formalized and routine, and there is a strong adherence to rules and policies.

Scores above 31 on this measure suggest that you prefer bureaucratic organizations, while scores below 17 suggest that you prefer organizations that are more informal and flexible. Scores between 18 and 30 suggest that you don't have a clear preference for either type.

Bureaucratic organizations have their advantages and disadvantages. Advantages include the ability to perform tasks efficiently and with less reliance on individuals at lower levels of the organization to make important decisions (because rules substitute for discretion). Disadvantages include a sometimes obsessive reliance on rules and policies, which greatly limits flexibility. In addition, bureaucratic organizations are not a good fit for cross-functional, self-managed teams, which organizations such as Motorola have used to promote innovation and creativity.

IV.G.1: How Much Do I Know About Organizational Behavior?

Instrument
Below are a number of statements about research findings in organizational behavior. For each statement, indicate whether you think it is true or false.

0=false
1=true

50. Leadership training is ineffective because good leaders are born, not made.
51. The most important requirement for an effective leader is to have an outgoing, enthusiastic personality.
52. Once employees have mastered a task, they perform better when they are told to "do their best" than when they are given specific, difficult performance goals.
53. On average, encouraging employees to participate in decision making is more effective for improving organizational performance than setting performance goals.
54. Teams with members from different functional areas are likely to reach better solutions to complex problems than teams from a single area.
55. There is very little difference among personality measures in terms of how well they predict an applicant's likely job performance.
56. Being very intelligent is actually a disadvantage for performing well on a low-skilled job.
57. Companies that screen job applicants for values have higher performance than those that screen for intelligence.
58. Groups tend to arrive at decisions faster than individuals on simple tasks.
59. When negotiating with another person, it's more effective to let the other person make the first offer because it reveals what the other person wants.
60. Employees who feel that they have been treated unfairly by their employer tend to steal more than employees who feel that they have been treated fairly.
61. A happy worker is not a productive worker.

Source: *Based on:* S. L. Rynes, A. E. Colbert, and K. G. Brown, "HR Professionals' Beliefs About Effective Human Resource Practices: Correspondence Between Research and Practice," *Human Resource Management*, (Summer, 2002), pp. 149-174.

Scoring Key
To score the measure, compute the number of correct responses. Correct answers to the 12 questions are as follows: 1: False (0), 2: False (0), 3: False (0), 4: False (0), 5: True (1), 6: False (0), 7: False (0), 8: False (0), 9: False (0), 10: False (0), 11: True (1), 12: False (0). Compute whether each response matches the correct response; matches should be counted as one, while discrepancies should be counted as zero. Scores will range from zero (all responses incorrect) to 12 (all responses correct).

Analysis and Interpretation
How much do you know about organizational behavior? That's what this scale measures. Your score can range from zero to 12, where 12 is a perfect score. If you aced this test, you can

congratulate yourself, but there is still a lot to learn – the above questions represent only a small part of the field of organizational behavior.

If you didn't score that well, don't worry. Many people come to a class on organizational behavior with preconceived notions that they believe are true. This is different than what you probably experienced in classes such as calculus or organic chemistry, where you came in without a lot of "facts" about the class. You'll find that some of your preconceived notions hold, while others don't.

Many of your preconceived notions may be based on common sense. Common sense tells us things such as "two heads are better than one," "opposites attract," and "a happy worker is a productive worker." Sometimes, research supports common wisdom and tells us what we thought we already knew. Other times, research is directly opposite to what we believe to be common sense. Many times, research tells us that the answer "depends." The interesting part comes when we understand exactly what the answer depends on, and research can tell us that, too. Thus, relying solely on common sense can be problematic.

The field of organizational behavior has been built from decades of research. Flip to the end of each chapter sometime and look at the endnotes – you'll find numerous citations of studies that generated the content of this book. As you go through this book, note the instances where the research tells you something you didn't know before; you may be surprised at how many times this will happen!

IV.G.2: How Much Do I Know About HRM?

Instrument
Below are a number of statements about research findings in human resource management. For each statement, indicate whether you think it is true or false.

0=false
1=true

62. Most managers give employees lower performance appraisals than they objectively deserve.
63. Poor performers are generally more realistic about their performance than good performers are.
64. Despite the popularity of drug testing, there is no clear evidence that applicants who score positive on drug tests are any less reliable or less productive employees.
65. Most people over-evaluate how well they perform on the job.
66. The most important determinant of how much training employees actually use on their jobs is how much they learned during training.
67. The most valid employment interviews are designed around each candidate's unique background.
68. Although there are "integrity tests" that try to predict whether someone will steal, be absent, or otherwise take advantage of an employer, they don't work well in practice because so many people lie on them.
69. On average, conscientiousness is a better predictor of job performance than is intelligence.
70. Most employees prefer to be paid on the basis of individual performance rather than on team or organizational performance.
71. There is a positive relationship between the proportion of managers receiving organizationally-based pay incentives and company profitability.

_____

Source: *Based on:* S. L. Rynes, A. E. Colbert, and K. G. Brown, "HR Professionals' Beliefs About Effective Human Resource Practices: Correspondence Between Research and Practice," *Human Resource Management*, (Summer, 2002), pp. 149-174.

Scoring Key
To score the measure, compute the number of correct responses. Correct answers to the 10 questions are as follows: 1: False (0), 2: False (0), 3: False (0), 4: True (1), 5: False (0), 6: False (0), 7: False (0), 8: False (0), 9: True (1), 10: True (1). Compute whether each response matches the correct response; matches should be counted as one, while discrepancies should be counted as zero. Scores will range from zero (all responses incorrect) to 10 (all responses correct).

Analysis and Interpretation
This scale measures how much you know about human resource management. Your score can range from zero to 10, where 10 is a perfect score. Although this measure assesses some key findings within the field of human resource management, there are many other important things to know.

If you didn't achieve a high score, don't worry just yet. These questions were given to nearly 1,000 human resource (HR) professionals in a variety of organizations. The professionals had an average of 14 years of work experience in human resource management. How did they do? On some of the questions (e.g., "Most managers give employees lower performance appraisals than they objectively deserve"), the vast majority gave the correct answer (which is "false," by the way). On other questions, however, a much smaller percentage gave the correct answer. For example, for the statement: "On average, conscientiousness is a better predictor of job performance than is intelligence," only 18% of the HR professionals gave the correct response (false)!

Why the discrepancies? There are several reasons. It could be that practicing HR professionals are unaware of research findings, either because they don't have time to read academic journals, or because the journals are so technically complex that it's too difficult to extract the main findings. It also could be that practicing HR professionals are aware of the research findings but choose not to utilize them because of factors such as political reasons, organizational inertia, or aversion to risk. In any event, closing the gap between research and practice is likely to be beneficial, as research has indicated that organizations who implement effective human resource management practices perform better than those that do not.

READ THIS LICENSE CAREFULLY BEFORE OPENING THIS PACKAGE. BY OPENING THIS PACKAGE, YOU ARE AGREEING TO THE TERMS AND CONDITIONS OF THIS LICENSE. IF YOU DO NOT AGREE, DO NOT OPEN THE PACKAGE. PROMPTLY RETURN THE UNOPENED PACKAGE AND ALL ACCOMPANYING ITEMS TO THE PLACE YOU OBTAINED THEM FOR A FULL REFUND OF ANY SUMS YOU HAVE PAID FOR THE SOFTWARE. *THESE TERMS APPLY TO ALL LICENSED SOFTWARE ON THE DISK EXCEPT THAT THE TERMS FOR USE OF ANY SHAREWARE OR FREEWARE ON THE DISKETTES ARE AS SET FORTH IN THE ELECTRONIC LICENSE LOCATED ON THE CD-ROM:*

1. **GRANT OF LICENSE and OWNERSHIP:** The enclosed computer programs and data ("Software") are licensed, not sold, to you by Pearson Education, Inc. publishing as Prentice-Hall, Inc. ("We" or the "Company") and in consideration of your purchase or adoption of the accompanying Company textbooks and/or other materials, and your agreement to these terms. We reserve any rights not granted to you. You own only the disk(s) but we and/or our licensors own the Software itself. This license allows you to use and display your copy of the Software on a single computer (i.e., with a single CPU) at a single location for <u>academic</u> use only, so long as you comply with the terms of this Agreement. You may make one copy for back up, or transfer your copy to another CPU, provided that the Software is usable on only one computer.

2. **RESTRICTIONS:** You may <u>not</u> transfer or distribute the Software or documentation to anyone else. Except for backup, you may <u>not</u> copy the documentation or the Software. You may <u>not</u> network the Software or otherwise use it on more than one computer or computer terminal at the same time. You may <u>not</u> reverse engineer, disassemble, decompile, modify, adapt, translate, or create derivative works based on the Software or the Documentation. You may be held legally responsible for any copying or copyright infringement that is caused by your failure to abide by the terms of these restrictions.

3. **TERMINATION:** This license is effective until terminated. This license will terminate automatically without notice from the Company if you fail to comply with any provisions or limitations of this license. Upon termination, you shall destroy the Documentation and all copies of the Software. All provisions of this Agreement as to limitation and disclaimer of warranties, limitation of liability, remedies or damages, and our ownership rights shall survive termination.

4. **LIMITED WARRANTY AND DISCLAIMER OF WARRANTY:** Company warrants that for a period of 60 days from the date purchase this SOFTWARE (or purchase or adopt the accompanying textbook), the Software, when properly installed and used in accordance with Documentation, will operate in substantial conformity with the description of the Software set forth in the Documentation, and that for a period of days the disk(s) on which the Software is delivered shall be free from defects in materials and workmanship under normal use. The Company do <u>not</u> warrant that the Software will meet your requirements or that the operation of the Software will be uninterrupted or error-free. Your only rem and the Company's only obligation under these limited warranties is, at the Company's option, return of the disk for a refund of any amounts paid it by you or replacement of the disk. THIS LIMITED WARRANTY IS THE ONLY WARRANTY PROVIDED BY THE COMPANY AND LICENSORS, AND THE COMPANY AND ITS LICENSORS DISCLAIM ALL OTHER WARRANTIES, EXPRESS OR IMPLIED, INCLUDI WITHOUT LIMITATION, THE IMPLIED WARRANTIES OF MERCHANTABILITY AND FITNESS FOR A PARTICULAR PURPOSE. T COMPANY DOES NOT WARRANT, GUARANTEE OR MAKE ANY REPRESENTATION REGARDING THE ACCURACY, RELIABILI CURRENTNESS, USE, OR RESULTS OF USE, OF THE SOFTWARE.

5. **LIMITATION OF REMEDIES AND DAMAGES:** IN NO EVENT, SHALL THE COMPANY OR ITS EMPLOYEES, AGENTS, LICENSORS, OR CONTRACTORS BE LIABLE FOR ANY INCIDENTAL, INDIRECT, SPECIAL, OR CONSEQUENTIAL DAMAGES ARISING OUT OF OR IN CONNECTION WITH THIS LICENSE OR THE SOFTWARE, INCLUDING FOR LOSS OF USE, LOSS OF DATA, LOSS OF INCOME OR PROFIT, OR OTHER LOSSES, SUSTAINED AS A RESULT OF INJURY TO ANY PERSON, OR LOSS OF OR DAMAGE TO PROPERTY, OR CLAIMS OF THIRD PARTIES, EVEN IF THE COMPANY OR AN AUTHORIZED REPRESENTATIVE OF THE COMPANY HAS BEEN ADVISED OF THE POSSIBILITY OF SUCH DAMAGES. IN NO EVENT SHALL THE LIABILITY OF THE COMPANY FOR DAMAGES WITH RESPECT TO THE SOFTWARE EXCEED THE AMOUNTS ACTUALLY PAID BY YOU, IF ANY, FOR THE SOFTWARE OR THE ACCOMPANYING TEXTBOOK. BECAUSE SOME JURISDICTIONS DO NOT ALLOW THE LIMITATION OF LIABILITY IN CERTAIN CIRCUMSTANCES, THE ABOVE LIMITATIONS MAY NOT ALWAYS APPLY TO YOU.

6. **GENERAL:** THIS AGREEMENT SHALL BE CONSTRUED IN ACCORDANCE WITH THE LAWS OF THE UNITED STATES O AMERICA AND THE STATE OF NEW YORK, APPLICABLE TO CONTRACTS MADE IN NEW YORK, AND SHALL BENEFIT THE COMPANY, ITS AFFILIATES AND ASSIGNEES. HIS AGREEMENT IS THE COMPLETE AND EXCLUSIVE STATEMENT OF THE AGREEMENT BETWEEN YOU AND THE COMPANY AND SUPERSEDES ALL PROPOSALS OR PRIOR AGREEMENTS, ORAL, OR WRITTEN, AND ANY OTHER COMMUNICATIONS BETWEEN YOU AND THE COMPANY OR ANY REPRESENTATIVE OF THE COMPANY RELATING TO THE SUBJECT MATTER OF THIS AGREEMENT. If you are a U.S. Government user, this Software is licensed with "restricted rights" as set forth in subparagraphs (a)-(d) of the Commercial Computer-Restricted Rights clause at FAR 52.227-19 or in subparagraphs (c)(1)(ii) of the Rights in Technical Data and Computer Software clause at DFARS 252.227-7013, and similar clauses, as applicable.

Should you have any questions concerning this agreement or if you wish to contact the Company for any reason, please contact in writing: Director of New Media, Higher Education Division, Prentice Hall, Inc., Upper Saddle River, NJ 07458